Jack hollered to me, "I can't hold it any longer. We're going down. Everyone bail out now!" He turned the ship inland. Everyone headed for the bomb bay.

I went on the cat walk, streams of gasoline pouring out of punctured lines, strapping on my chest pack chute, and then hesitated as I looked out into that open space below me. In that brief instant of time where I was hesitating, wondering whether to go down with the ship or trust the piece of silk strapped to my chest, I felt a nudge of a foot in my back and I was committed to space.

I was amazed at the sensation. It did not feel like I was falling. I was just lying back on a cushion of air, no sound of wind rushing by, no sound at all. We had never received actual training on parachuting, only lectures. We were told to count to ten before pulling the rip cord. I had only counted to three, but I could see the plane was far away. I said, "To hell with this," and I pulled. Nothing happened. Panic set in! How long had this chute been stuffed in this pouch since it was last repacked?

Also from Storyteller Press

Midnight in Never Land
by Perry Bradford Wilson & Michael Norris

Tales of McKinleyville:
Big Doin's at the Chinese Baptist Church
by Perry Bradford Wilson

Tales of Placerville:
Bradford & Norris, Booksellers to the Savage West
by Perry Bradford Wilson

visit us at storytellerpress.com

Everyday P.O.W.

By Bradford P. Wilson

Edited by Perry Bradford Wilson

STORYTELLER PRESS
Pollock Pines, CA

Everyday P.O.W.

© 2010 by Perry Bradford Wilson

All rights reserved under International and Pan-American Copyright Conventions. Without limiting the rights under copyright reserved above, no part of this book may be reproduced or transmitted in any form or by any means, electronic or mechanical, including photocopying, recording, or by any information storage and retrieval system, without permission in writing from the author.

Published in the United States by
Storyteller Press
5774 Sierra Springs Drive
Pollock Pines, CA 95726

http://www.storytellerpress.com/

ISBN 1-880053-03-9
First Printed Edition, September 2010
First Digital Edition, October 2010

Library of Congress Cataloging-in-Publication Data is available from the publisher.
Book design & illustrations by Perry Bradford Wilson

Table of Contents

Introduction	1
Prologue - September 12, 1944	5
1 Son of Three Sisters	13
2 December 7, 1941	41
3 Primary Training, 1943	59
4 Navigation, 1943	64
5 Across The Sea, 1944	72
6 The 445th, 1944	83
7 Barbara, 1944	98
8 Prisoner of War, 1944	109
9 The Long Wait, 1944	161
10 The End of Stalag Luft 1	168
11 The Trip Home, 1945	178
12 An Anniversary	195
Afterword	198
Photos & Illustrations	*123*
Map	*next page*

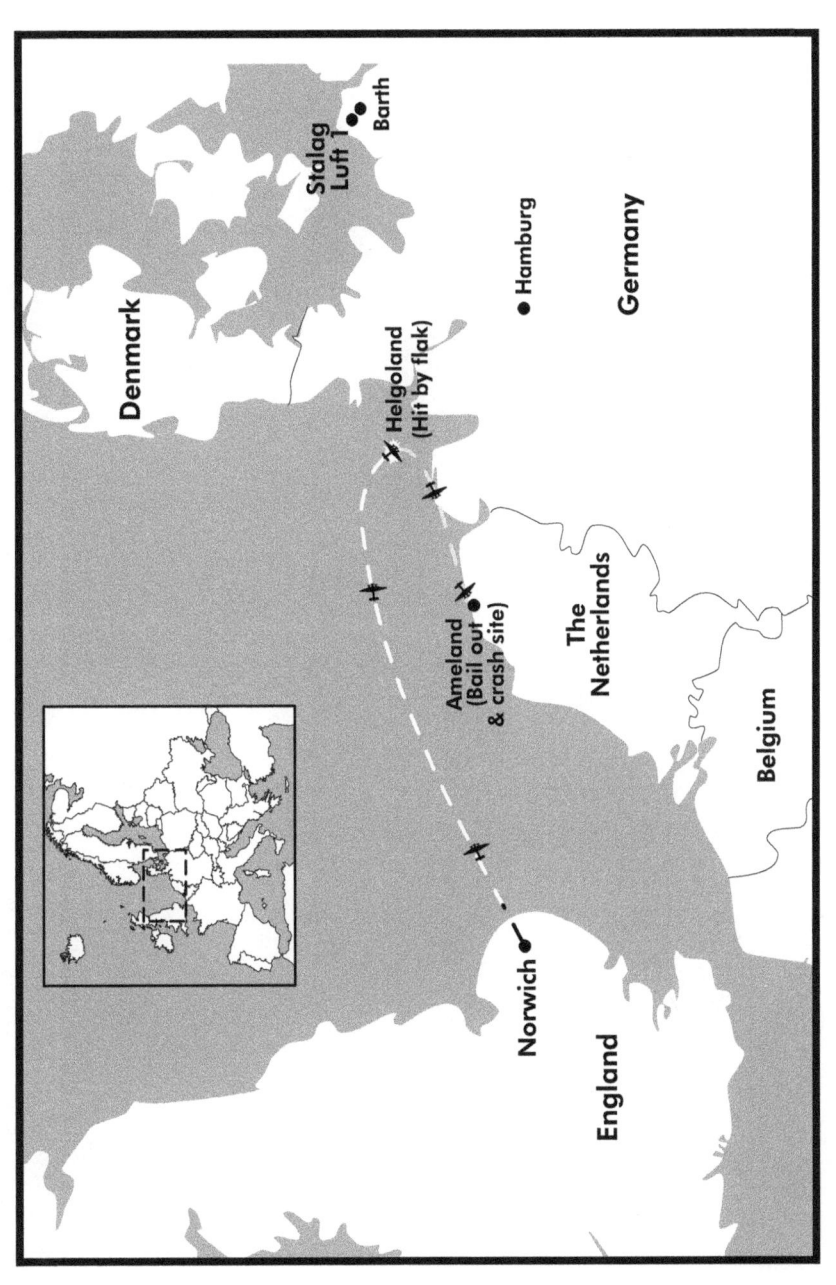

Introduction
by Perry Bradford Wilson

Almost every Saturday morning throughout my childhood my family sat around the breakfast table after we finished the double-helping of pancakes, waffles or French toast (the "syrup breakfasts," as we called them) that my dad had made for us, and we talked. If we didn't have any major weekend plans these after-breakfast conversations could last two or three hours. My brother, sister and I talked about our school week. My mother talked about her week. But my father didn't talk about work.

Not that his job wasn't interesting – he worked first for NASA, and then later as a civilian administrator for the cumbersomely-named Army Air Mobility Research and Development Laboratory. Personally, I thought the huge hangers and wind tunnels at Ames Research Center were fascinating. But my dad worked in the number-crunching end and didn't have much to say about work. Instead he talked about the world at large.

He talked politics, science, pop culture; whatever came to mind. It was always fascinating, because he never pontificated. He just threw out ideas, many of them hilariously funny, and we learned from him.

On many occasions he talked about his childhood in the rural California communities of Almaden and Redwood Valley during the Great Depression. He didn't particularly like to talk about himself – he had no issues of ego. These talks weren't overly wistful reminiscences, either. Usually they were framed in a historical context; the fallout of World War I, the changes in technology, the fallout of the Depression, the world stage and coming of World War II. Yet these events were described in a personal context that defined them in a relatable way.

As a student fascinated by history (and just about anything else) I loved these Saturday morning talks. However, as I got older I noticed something. The survey of history usually ended at the beginning of World War II and then picked up again after the war was over. When he did talk about the war it was in bold strokes that painted the same information we learned at school. Before and after the war his history was personal. During the war it was factual. In fact, my mother's stories of how her family dealt with rationing and other home front issues during the war were far more personal than anything my dad said.

My siblings and I already knew the general outline of his wartime experiences; my father was a navigator in the Army Air Corps during the war. He was shot down over Germany and spent the better part of a year in P.O.W. camp. But beyond these facts the details were always sketchy.

Finally one Saturday morning I asked him directly about it. Was he uncomfortable talking about it? "No," he said, although he didn't explain why he hadn't bothered to bring it up. "I was just an everyday P.O.W.," he added. Then he proceeded to tell us his story in more detail than ever before.

Over time he finally seemed to exhaust the subject but I was always curious for more details. Since I missed Vietnam (by a handful of years) and was too old by the time Bosnia and the various Gulf conflicts arose, I never had to think about serving during a "hot" war. Safe and sound in California it was hard to imagine being put in harm's way at such a young age. How did all those average Joes cope with sudden immersion in armed conflict? In college I interviewed my Dad on camera about his war experiences for a broadcasting class project. I recorded several hours of audio interviews with him a few years later.

Finally, in the late 1990s, I suggested to my father that he should write some of this down himself, in his own words. A young Belgian man named Luc Dewez had likewise been pressing him to write some of his experiences down. Luc was gathering information about the 8th Air Force and the war from his country's perspective. At last my dad gave in and started writing.

Once in a while he e-mailed me a chapter or two and asked me what I thought. The manuscript was just what I hoped it would be; not a history lesson, but a recollection of how one rural California boy made it – one day at a time – through challenging circumstances. I promised him that if he didn't try getting it published then I certainly would.

After his death in December 2007 I sorted through the files on my father's computer (at the age of 86 he was very computer literate) and found the manuscript he had been working on. It was unfinished, but most of the story was there. In addition I had many other resources he had shared with me. As the unofficial "family historian" he had given me boxes of old photographs, including the actual journals he wrote while in prison camp and the telegrams his parents received from the War Department.

So I kept my promise. Here, with minimal editing in order to keep the text in his words as much as possible, is his story. There are some jumps from time to time – bridging sections he meant, I am sure, to fill in later. I've tried to smooth over these transitions without altering the substance of the manuscript.

When I read these pages I still marvel at how my father took each new event in stride and wonder how I would match up in similar circumstances. I suppose we all rise to the occasion when pressed, but I think (and I am, of course, biased) that he was an exceptional individual.

NOTE

LETTERS HOME

From the time he joined the Army through the day he was shot down and became a prisoner of war, my father regularly wrote letters home to his parents. Excerpts from these letters are presented boxed in italics with the header "Letter Home." Each of these was written on the date noted.

Brad Wilson's STALAG LUFT 1 P.O.W. JOURNAL, 1945

During the months of January, 1945 through May, 1945 my father kept a diary or journal while he was incarcerated in Stalag Luft 1 as a prisoner of war. They are hand written by pencil in a "blue book" sort of slim stapled paper booklet. There are pages where it is clear there was writing that he erased, presumably in order to reuse the paper, which was at a premium. I wonder what those long-ago erased passages said.

Some of the entries in his journal concern what was currently taking place and others are memories of what had happened in the past. Rather than print the journal verbatim (which would result in lots of "roll call, ate, ate, roll call, ate, slept" sorts of entries) I have decided to include entries from the journal throughout this book, placed with their subject matter. So while the bulk of the text in this book was written in the early 2000s (and is only as best as my father's memory served at that time) the pieces presented in this manner (boxed in italics) with the header "Brad Wilson's Stalag Luft 1 P.O.W. Journal" were actually written in 1945 while he was in prison camp. Certainly at that time his memories were more immediate.

Prologue
September 12, 1944

Summer in Great Britain was rapidly drawing to a close. We had just gone through three months of mild weather, lots of clouds, some sunshine, but none of the hot weather that I was used to back in California. If this is summer, I wondered, what will their winter bring? We had just been briefed on our latest mission, delivering heavy bombs to Hamburg, and I was on the way out to the air strip in the back of the "covered wagon" Army truck that strongly resembled the covered wagons of the old west - only having an engine up front where the horses should be. Along for the ride were most of my crew members as well as other planes' crew members. There was no banter as we bumped along the tarmac. The truck dropped us off near our plane and moved on to the next. We entered the bomb bay of the B-24 assigned to us that day. It appeared to be a brand new model right in from the states. On the nose was the inevitable art work with the name *Dixie Flyer* in brilliant yellow and orange. The crew that created that nose art and flew the ship over from the states may have been assigned to another group somewhere, and here we were flying their beautiful new ship. But that was life in the good old US Army Air Force.

I grunted as I crawled through the narrow tunnel, past the "putt-putt" motor which was used to start the engines, and up into the navigator's compartment. Teddy, my bombardier, wiggled through the tight quarters and entered the nose turret. I went through the process of hooking up, checked to see that my parachute and flak helmet were where they belonged, and got out the "tools of my trade" and spread them on my desk. These tools included an E-6B computer, which was a rather wider and more complicated instrument than a slide rule, but had nothing in common with the instruments we now refer to as "computers," since they hadn't been invented yet. Through some calculations with my E-6B, good accurate wind speeds from our weather briefing, some careful plotting on my map, and careful timing of our flight in progress, I was usually able to keep our position pretty well defined. Throwing in an occasional check of my G-box - when in range - I could usually pinpoint our location.

Teddy rode in the nose turret position, since bombardiers dropped their bombs based on the lead ship's drop and didn't use their independent bomb sight. In a case where the lead ship was disabled, then the next ship assigned to take over would move in place and that bombardier would use his bomb sight to zero in on the target. That meant that we had only a nine man crew. If the bombardier was assigned to his regular duties, an additional gunner would be added to the nose turret.

The crew chief started the "putt putt," which was a good indication that we would soon be airborne. This small gasoline engine ran the generator which provided the power to start the engines. After a few minutes we heard a sharp whine as number one engine turned over, and then the soft whir of the propeller as it gained speed. This was followed by each engine in succession until the roar became deafening. After a few minutes the pilot said to prepare for takeoff, so Teddy and I joined them on the flight deck. This meant disengaging ourselves from our various connections temporarily. We crawled through the tunnel again, faithfully lugging our parachutes with us as we went. You never moved anywhere in the plane when it was airborne without your parachute at your side. There might not be a second chance to go back and get it.

We taxied out onto the strip and lined up with the other 30

or more planes that were flying from our group that day. Teddy and I were flying with Webster and his crew. This was possibly the last flight with Web before being reassigned back to fly with our original crew - the one we flew over with from the states. Our first twelve flights had been with "Don" Donald and Frank Smith, the pilot and co-pilot we had joined back in Tucson, Arizona. Right now I was on my fifth flight with Webster.

    We first met Webster in the confines of our Quonset hut where he bunked along with the officers of his crew and three other crews. We referred to him as "Web," although his regular crew mates called him "Skip." Web was a little wilder and more reckless than Don. In fact, on one occasion he was flying the "slot" position in our squadron formation, which is directly behind the lead ship. They had dropped their bombs and were on the way home and it was a rather boring flight. So, Web decided to have some fun with the lead ship. Regulations required keeping a "safe" distance from other ships in the formation, but he decided he was going to see if he could get right up behind the rear gun turret on the lead ship. His plane was flying slightly below the lead ship, so he wasn't in its slip stream. He kept nudging his plane closer and closer and Jack Sherman, his co-pilot, was getting slightly nervous. In the lead ship, the tail gunner was having a nervous fit. He called his pilot on the intercom and told him what was going on. His pilot couldn't do anything about it, because inter-plane communication over enemy territory was forbidden. Finally, the gunner called his pilot and said, "If that son of a bitch gets any closer, I'm going to shoot him down!" He moved his guns menacingly toward Webster's ship. I think Webster got the idea and gradually dropped back. I heard later that he had a "discussion" with the group CO following that episode.

    After the usual delay, we finally taxied into position on the runway, the engines roared and the plane rushed down the runway as if eager to get airborne and be on the way with its heavy load of 500 pound bombs. It took the best part of an hour to get the planes in formation. The lead pilot flew in a large circle around a beacon and the last planes to take off would fall into place and we'd head off over the English Channel. During this circling time, Teddy and I would return to our stations and hook up again. At 27,000 feet, which was our flight altitude, things could get pretty cold. So, in addition to electric boots and an electric suit to keep us warm, we also had electric gloves. I had learned how to write and plot my courses on the map with these gloves on. They were so thick it made for rather clumsy work. After those electrical connections were made, we plugged in our oxygen masks, our throat mikes, our ear phones, and settled in for a long ride.

Today we were flying in the slot position in our squadron, which meant we were directly behind the lead plane. It was not a good place to be if they were shooting flak at you. It seems the German gunners generally aimed for the lead plane, but somehow the explosions were always just late enough that they would catch the plane in the slot instead. This was an uncomfortable thought as we headed out over the sea.

We were supposed to fly a path over the North Sea that day which would take us past the Danish Peninsula, then turn south until we were over land, then turn west and approach Hamburg from the east. I don't know why they planned this devious route, unless they thought there was some element of surprise in it. At any rate, the Group's lead navigator had other plans. We turned south just before we reached the Danish Peninsula, according to my calculations. There was a solid under cast of clouds as far as the eye could see, and, no way we could see any land. And, of course, there was no communication between ships allowed over enemy territory, so we had no idea if he knew what he was doing or not. I talked to the pilot and told him we were flying 90 miles west of our scheduled course, but there was nothing else to do about it. It was moments after that that we passed directly over the island of Helgoland, a German fortress that consisted of "wall to wall" flak batteries, and, as they say, that's when all hell broke loose!

I heard this strange sound like someone throwing gravel against the side of the plane. Then the plane went up on one wing and dived down out of formation before leveling off. I knew we'd been hit by flak, and looking out the port side I could see two dead engines with their props feathered. I heard the co-pilot's voice on the intercom—"Brad, Brad, give me a heading!" My intercom didn't work. Just then the doors to the nose turret flung open and hit me in the back. Teddy came tumbling out shouting, "What da we do? What da we do?" We had been so thoroughly briefed on what to expect if we had to ditch the ship over water, that I automatically said, "Salvo the bombs! Go back to the bomb bay and rig the restraints for ditching." He pulled the salvo lever that opened the bomb bay doors and dropped the bombs, and headed for the tunnel, parachute in hand. I grabbed my map, ripped off my connections, grabbed my parachute, and scrambled through the tunnel after him, then turned up to the flight deck. Webster was sitting on the bench behind the pilot's seat with the radio operator trying to bandage his legs which were bleeding profusely. Jack Sherman, the co-pilot, was trying to fly the B-24 on two engines and struggling with the controls to keep it aloft. I told him to take a heading due west. There was nothing south of us but German coast covered with flak batteries. We headed west, our hope being that we might possibly get back as far as Antwerp which was, I believed, in Allied hands by this time. Jack did one hell of a fine job keeping that plane up as long as he did. All along the coast, which was now visible through broken clouds, you could see puffs of flak explosions as the gunners continued shooting at us. We had lowered our landing gear, which was supposed to be an international distress signal that we were going down. But they continued using us for target practice.

We reached a point on the map where we were off the North Coast of Holland. We didn't want to cut across the land - too many flak batteries - so we continued west, planning to turn south on the far side of Holland. Jack hollered to me, "I can't hold it any longer. We're going down. Everyone bail out now!" He turned the ship inland over Ameland Island. Everyone headed for the bomb bay.

I went out on the cat walk, streams of gasoline pouring out of punctured lines somewhere, strapping on my chest pack chute, and then hesitated as I looked out into that open space below me. In that brief instant of time where I was hesitating, wondering whether to go down with the ship or trust the piece of silk strapped to my chest, I felt a nudge of a foot in my back and I was committed to space. I was amazed at the sensation. It did not feel like I was falling. I was just lying back on a cushion of air, no sound of wind rushing by, no sound at all. We had never received actual training on parachuting, only lectures. We were told to count to ten before pulling the rip cord. I had only counted to three, but I could see the plane was far away. I said, "To hell with this," and I pulled. Nothing happened. Panic set in! How long had this chute been stuffed in this pouch since it was last repacked?

I reached in and started digging. I pulled the drogue chute out by hand and the rest followed. With a slight jerk I was suddenly floating down to Earth. I was grateful that I wasn't wearing a back pack chute - if the rip cord had failed I wouldn't have been able to pull it out by hand!

Other parachutes hung in the sky around me. I did not feel like I was dropping very rapidly. It was as though I was just hanging up there on a huge sky hook. Then some sappy German soldiers, or possibly civilians, started shooting at us with rifles. I could hear the bullets whistling by. I was not in the mood to hang there like a sitting duck. I remembered a lecture about "slipping the chute to get it to drop more rapidly." A very bad idea, but I was in a hurry to get down. I tugged at one side and nothing happened, fortunately. But, by this time it looked like I was getting reasonably close, so I gave up tugging, and started stretching, reaching with my toes for good old solid ground. Gone were all memories of our lectures about how to land properly. Only panic remained. I wanted DOWN before I was shot. There was a barbed wire fence only about six feet away from the spot I was aiming for. If I hit the barbed wire, I thought, it could just about cut me in half. I hit with such an impact that, I found out later, I crushed a disk in my spine. My lungs collapsed completely and I couldn't take in a breath of air. As I folded up on the ground I thought I was dead or dying at least.

A Luftwaffe soldier was standing over me with a rifle, shaking it menacingly as if I was a threat to him! Finally, while I was struggling for a breath of air, he frisked me to see if I was carrying a revolver. Satisfied that I was not, he rolled me over on my back.

"For you, the war is over," he said in clear English. This was, I learned later, something the soldiers were taught to say to captured airmen, perhaps to take some of the vinegar out of them. After what seemed an eternity I was able to take in a little air, and then a little more, until I was able to breathe again. He helped me up and I limped across an open field to a spot where other soldiers had already rounded up Web, Jack, our radio operator and our engineer. We all sat on the ground, glum and silent. Teddy and the three gunners were not there.

So, I thought, for us the war is over. Perhaps it was, but it was only the beginning of the strange, frightening and sometimes surreal experience of being a prisoner of war. This was something I had never anticipated. Planes were shot down, crews bailed out, but that always happened to "the other guy." I had plans of finishing my bombing tour - after all, this was my seventeenth mission. I was just about half way to the required 35 missions before we would be returned to the states and a new assignment. In all those 17 missions we had never seen a German fighter plane. We had always flown too high for the flak to be a viable threat. Now it had proved to be our downfall.

1

Son of Three Sisters

In many ways we are our families, and never was that more true than in the Great Depression. The Depression destroyed many things and built up others. My family was one of them. My mother, her sisters and her parents had always been fairly close. The nation's financial troubles brought them together even closer for survival. We all came together in the small rural community of Redwood Valley, growing our own food, making ends meet, and helping each other get through hard times.

Today (as I write this) it is July 22, 2005. It is the 146th birthday of my grandfather August "Augie" Zeiler. He was born on July 22, 1859 and died in 1936. My first memory of Augie was when I was about 4 years old. He worked as a salesman for the barber supply house of Will & Finck in San Francisco. He drove a model T panel truck around the city delivering all the good stuff the barbers used in those days. He made a good salesman because he was an extremely friendly person and called everybody "neighbor." He was 6 feet tall, with a slim build, a big burly mustache, and thin white hair strands which he combed across the top of his head to keep from looking bald - and it worked!

In spite of the fact that he worked for a barber supply house, he never quite got the hang of shaving. He had a three to four - inch wide razor strap that he "stropped" his straight edge razor on every morning. He lathered up his face with a big brush in a lather cup and proceeded to scrape the beard off his face. Every morning he came out with little patches of toilet paper stuck on all the places he had nicked himself.

I can remember the little Model T Augie drove around San Francisco (a priceless relic today with gas lanterns for headlights.) Augie and Emily lived in a flat on Potrero in San Francisco when I was born in 1921. Then they moved to a big apartment on Nob Hill with us in about 1926. Later, when we moved to Almaden near San Jose, they moved into a flat on Hampshire Street.

Augie and his wife Emily got along well *except* when they were moving. Then they always got in a hassle about setting up the stove in the new living quarters. I'm not clear on the nature of the disagreement, only that it was a sore subject and was never to be discussed. And, of course, they had little arguments over their toast each morning. In those days we didn't have automatic "pop-up" toasters. Em and Aug had to have toast every morning and every morning they expected the other one would watch the toaster. When I was staying with Augie and Em I always knew when breakfast was ready - I could hear Emily scratching the "burned" off the toast into the sink. I don't believe they ever had a piece of properly browned toast in their lives.

The biggest move they ever made was when they followed their three grown daughters - Adeline (aka "Bebe Snow"), Elsie, and Lenore (aka "Noan" or "Nony") from Alma, Wisconsin to San Francisco, California. It turned out to be a good move for them, though, and Augie enjoyed his years working for Will & Finck.

Eventually age and ill health caught up with Augie and he had to quit work. The next year they moved to Almaden briefly with my mother and father and I, and then up to Redwood Valley, a beautiful part of the California coast range near Ukiah. Augie's beloved Model T was left behind in rust and ruin at Almaden when they moved to Redwood Valley.

My mother Noan, Augie's youngest daughter, built her parents a little house on property Augie owned across the vineyard from her sister Elsie and Elsie's husband Oscar. Nony paid for the building of the entire house out of the salary she made working for a wholesale candy company where she earned $10 per week. Augie lived in that house until he died in 1936. Emily then moved in with her daughter Bebe and Bebe's husband Nate in a refurbished schoolhouse they had moved into a few years earlier when Nate lost his job with the Hermann Safe Company.

Mt grandmother Emily was born on June 22, 1857, in Alma, Wisconsin and lived until 1944. She was not just my grandmother, she was also one of the sweetest people I ever knew.

I don't know much about her family, except that she was born Emma Kurtz in Alma. She had a brother named George who found his way to California and raised a big family in Fruitvale, an area of Oakland. I never saw Uncle George after the age of seven or eight, so I only have a child's memory of him and his family. George married a beautiful young woman (at least from her pictures) named Lydia who had the slim "wasp" waist that was all the rage in those days. But somehow she lost that shape soon after they were married and blossomed into a 300 pound matron who had three boys and three girls. All the girls took after their mama and each weighed in at close to 300 pounds! The boys apparently took after their dad. Uncle George looked a lot like Joseph Stalin, but he was a very kindly person. The big problem with Lydia and her three daughters was that they couldn't handle their weight very well - they smelled really bad. Whenever we went to visit them, which was at least three or four times a year (I don't know why we ever went since the smell in their house was so bad, except that George was Emily's brother and she felt she was obligated to visit him occasionally.) I dreaded going along. Unfortunately I was just a little kid at the time and didn't have a say in the matter. I'd try to "cut off" my sense of smell when we would first get there until my smell receptors got numb to the odor. By the time we would leave I couldn't smell anything, period. I don't remember that they were ever invited to come to our place. When we went to see them we rode across the bay on the ferry (the best part of the day), took the "Key" system of old red electric trains from the ferry slip to Fruitvale Avenue, and then walking about a block to their house. They served good food, and the table and the plates were clean, so we weren't afraid of "catching the smell". But we had to wash all our clothes when we got home. It was bad. Real bad!

In later years, just before Emily and Augie moved to Redwood Valley, George and Lydia and the girls and their husbands moved up there, too. The boys stayed in Oakland. George bought a small ranch and house named "The Wells Place". And no matter how many people bought it and moved in and out, it retained that name. Uncle George, as he was always called by us, built the little house for Noan that she erected for Emily and Augie to live in.

Emily worked very hard until Augie died. She had to carry all the water they used in a bucket or two from the spring, about 300 yards from the house. And taking care of Augie wasn't easy as he grew weaker by the day. After he was gone and she moved up to Bebe's schoolhouse, we all made sure she lived the "Life of Riley." Whenever Bebe and Noan went to town and left me home, I would head up the hill to Bebe's place to be with Emily. She was always so glad to see me coming that she would run in and start making me lunch even though I had just finished breakfast. I had to hold her down to keep her from cooking for me!

I knew during the war when I was in prison camp and had no communications from home that Emily wouldn't last till I got back. I wanted my letters to get through to her so badly I wrote to her weekly from prison camp, (we were only allowed to write one letter a week), but she never lived to get one of my letters, which were delivered shortly after the war when I got back home. She died shortly after the news was received that I was missing in action. To me, she was the most wonderful person on Earth.

Augie and Emily, as I said, had three daughters.

Bebe Snow (aka Adeline Elizabeth Zeiler Forbes) was the oldest of the three Zeiler sisters, born on January 27, 1883. After the war when my wife, Joy, and I were building our first house in Redwood Valley, she came over to see us and would sit on a chair and watch us build. She talked to us by the hour about the old days, much the same way I'm doing in these pages. I guess that's what old people do. We could never get enough of Bebe. We went up to her house and played cards and when we went to leave, we were always so busy talking about something interesting that we'd ask her to sit in the car with us - this is after we had already left the house and gotten into the car expecting to leave. We might end up talking for another hour..

She got the nickname "Bebe" when she was a child. Her favorite newspaper comic strip was called "Phoebe Snow," and Augie and Emily started calling her that. Somewhere along the line it got changed to "Bebe." She married Charles Nathan Forbes back in Minnesota and then the two of them were the first to pick up stakes and move to California. Nate was a traveling salesman at the time. He was never called Charles or Charlie, just "Nate" or (in Noan's case) "immer faulch" (correct spelling unknown) which meant "always mad." Bebe couldn't have children - reason unknown - although she would have made a great mother. I have a feeling old "immer faulch" would have been a bastard of a father.

I first remember Bebe living in a flat on Hampshire Street

in San Francisco. It was a large and spacious with hardwood floors and was beautifully furnished. Nate was then working for the Hermann Safe Company. He was a foreman - the kind you wouldn't like to have. Many times he would come home with skinned knuckles from having a fist fight with one of his employees. He said he knew how to keep them in line. Where was the human resources department when you needed them?? He also was unrelentingly racist. Noan used to say that he was a "piece of work." She also said "you don't pick your family."

When the depression came along, Nate lost his job and they moved up to Redwood Valley where they bought the old school house and a few acres of land. Nate went to work for the WPA. They built a huge chicken coop and raised chickens (over 500 of them at one time). Later, he built a machine shop and did repairs on farm equipment for the local farmers. They muddled through the depression like the rest of us did. Their friends from San Francisco would come up to see them frequently on weekends, and Bebe kept busy killing fryers and making meals for her guests until she finally got so tired of it that she didn't ask them back anymore. It was great for the guests–a nice weekend in the country, free meals, and good company. But things were in short supply and they probably didn't realize that Bebe was skimping to make ends meet just to feed them. Lucky they had the fryers.

They had a brick lined well that was their water supply. The electric pump was situated in a cellar dug into the ground adjacent to the well. On the top of the well was an old fashioned hand pump used for emergencies, like when the electricity went out. Well, one summer they had a bevy of guests, as usual, and the water in the well had acquired an unusual taste. Nate passed it off to his guests as being part of a mineral spring that fed the well. All his guests were quite thrilled and drank copious amounts of his "mineral water", which they decided was good for their health. After the guests had gone home, Nate went down to the well to see what the "real" source of this new mineral water was. He discovered that some of the bricks in the wall had fallen in at the level of the cellar along with a big old snake which was floating on the surface pretty well decomposed by that time. Neither he nor Bebe ever told the guests.

They remodeled the old school house slowly and by 1940, it was a very comfortable home. It started with one huge room with 12 foot ceilings. This he subdivided into four large rooms, a bath, and a hall. In addition, the "cloak room" he converted into a dinette and the kitchen was built on top of part of the outside deck that surrounded the house. This took place before plywood, before sheetrock, and before a lot of the building materials we have today. The walls dividing the rooms were made of 1x6 fir nailed diagonally across the studs and covered by building paper to keep the draft out. A few years later he lowered the ceilings to 8 feet and made the house into a pretty decent home. The fireplace that Nate built is a story in itself. Nate didn't want just the ordinary fireplace; he wanted to design it himself. So, he built a wooden form in the shape of the fireplace he wanted. Then he mixed concrete and poured the form full. It measured about five feet high by at least six feet wide and eight inches deep. When it was thoroughly set he - all by himself - lifted the form with the concrete in it to a vertical position. He would never admit that he couldn't lift it alone, so he did it by himself. I have no idea how he got that much weight up off the floor. And the result was not great; a gray concrete fireplace, with indentations here and there from the form. He also poured a concrete chimney that rose at least 15 feet from the ground. He carried every ounce of concrete up a ladder and poured it into the form he had built!

Elsie Zeiler was the middle sister of the three Zeiler girls. She met and married Oscar Huber while they still lived in Wisconsin. They had a daughter, Virginia, November 24, 1910, in Alma. Virginia was my only cousin, and as I had no brothers and sisters she was the only other "kid" in the family - and eleven years older than me at that. Elsie, Oscar and Virginia eventually followed Bebe and Nate to California. They all started out in San Francisco, but as the depression made things harder to live in the city they made a trip to Ukiah and got interested in some property in Redwood Valley. Oscar and Elsie wanted to run a ranch and there were a large number of acres available, but it was more than Elsie and Oscar could afford to handle alone. After some deliberating the family went together on the purchase. Augie and Emily bought 3 acres, including a 2 acre vineyard of Mission grapes; Nate bought 10 acres plus the old school house and its adjoining grounds; and Oscar and Elsie ended up with a 63 acre farm. As often happens with these sorts of arrangements, there was a big family dispute on how it all was handled and Nate ended up refusing to talk, visit, or look at Oscar. This was hard on Bebe, because she couldn't even visit the rest of the family on Christmas and other occasions where Oscar was present. This went on for more than 10 years.

Elsie and Oscar planted around 27 acres of grapes, 10 acres of pears, and had a "family orchard" of apples, plums, pears, walnuts, and other delightful items, adjoining their house. Behind the barn were 2 acres that were planted to corn each year. Closer to the house was a garden where they raised most of their food. They had two horses, (one, an old plow horse, and one a showy pinto that Oscar liked to ride in parades in Ukiah each year). They also had two milk cows. So this was a real ranch/farm. It was also the depression and to make ends meet Oscar cut firewood for sale. They had over 10 acres of land covered with manzanita, madrone, oak and firs. Oscar cut a lot of manzanita and madrone and dragged it with his tractor down below the house where he had a one-cylinder gasoline buck saw. To cut the wood, you had to lift the long limbs up onto a sliding table and then push the table so that the limb would go through the whirring 16 to 18 inch saw blade. The old one-cylinder made an ungodly sound as it putt-putted its way through the logs. Since the logs were quite heavy, Oscar lifted them up onto the table and balanced them while Elsie pushed the table through the blade. She did this for many years, and died an early death in 1934. Oscar lived until 1943 but died sometime while I was overseas. They both passed on in their late forties or early fifties.

I became quite familiar with the firewood business as I was hired to stack the cut wood into tiers and cords. I got 10 cents a tier. On a good day, I could maybe earn 30 cents. But mostly I petered out before I got that far. (I was 10 years old at the time). Those were the summers I spent "up on the ranch" with Aunt Elsie and Uncle Oscar while we were still living in Almaden.

The summers on the ranch were wonderful. That's when I first became acquainted with the old swimming hole. Also, the barn was full in the summertime with new mown hay, and I used to crawl up in the rafters and jump down into the mountain of hay. The dust would rise, but it had such a good smell to it! Collecting eggs was almost like an Easter egg hunt. The chickens had the run of the barnyard and the barn. Although they had nests built for them in the chicken coop and actually used some of them, often they would wander off into the barn, climb up into the hay and build a nest there for laying their eggs. When you found these nests, you would always have to leave a "nest egg" to fool the chicken into thinking that was what she had laid the day before. Then she would continue to lay eggs there. Otherwise, she would saunter off and build a new nest that you might not find. Sometimes the nest eggs were made of glass, but the chicken didn't know the difference. It was fun finding a new nest which might have eight or ten eggs in it. But I had to make sure I discovered them as soon as possible or the eggs would spoil. Every once in a while a hen would decide it was time to raise a brood. Then she would sit on the nest and wouldn't leave it at all. So I would have to lift her up and swipe the eggs from underneath. She didn't like that and would peck at me and make an awful fuss. I let Aunt Elsie handle the setters.

One day Aunt Elsie got on old Fanny and I got on Paint and we headed up towards the flat. Fanny was an old plow horse and plodded along at a leisurely pace. Paint was a beautiful brown and white pinto and was very feisty. I should have been on old Fanny. We started up the steep driveway beside the house and leveled out as the road past the vineyard and the infamous ten acres that belonged to Nate. Paint kept tossing his head and was going along at a pretty good trot and Fanny was picking up the rear a ways back. Suddenly, Paint decided this was not a good time to go walking, so he just reared up, turned around and started heading back the road leading down to the house and then on to the barn. I couldn't get him to stop and I called, "Auntie, Auntie!" Well, Elsie turned old Fanny around and was galloping as fast as that old horse would go but couldn't catch up. When we got to the steep road going down past the house, Paint never slowed down. I was going lickety-split and it was all I could do to stay in the saddle. I was gripping the sides of the horse with my legs as best as I could, and holding onto the saddle horn for dear life. Paint plunged down the second hill to the barnyard and then came to an abrupt halt at the fence. I don't know how I kept from flying over his head and over the fence. Moments later, Aunt Elsie arrived on Fanny and helped me down. Oscar came up and took Paint's reins. Then he took off his hat and swatted Paint a few times right on the nose and used some choice cuss words to let him know he'd done wrong! My legs were shaking so badly from the adrenaline rush that I could hardly walk. I went up to the front porch of the house that overlooked the barn and the barnyard and sat on the couch for about an hour. I watched as Oscar tossed a few more cuss words at Paint and then he got into the saddle and yanked the horse's reins around and showed him that when he was told to go a certain direction, that was where he was going to go. It was quite a while before Paint got back to the barn again.

Oscar didn't mind cutting corners now and then, sometimes to his own dismay. He had an old Model T truck that he used on the farm and Augie asked him to come down to San Francisco and pick up a load of furniture he wanted to haul to Redwood Valley. Oscar agreed, but his brakes on the old Model T were not in top condition. Augie gave him money to get the brakes fixed before the trip. Well, Oscar wondered how bad the brakes really were, so he stepped hard on them and the truck stopped nicely. He proceeded to pocket the money and head out for Redwood Valley with Noan on board. She was going up to be with Elsie for a few days and thought she'd save the cost of the train by riding up with Oscar. In those days, the road from Cloverdale to Hopland was called the "Cloverdale Grade." This was before the "river road" was built. It was very steep, twisty and corkscrewed around the mountain. Oscar and Noan reached the summit and started down the twisty road when they came up on another car going very slowly. Oscar stepped on the brakes to slow down so that he wouldn't run into the car in front of them. Nothing happened. He kept pushing on the brakes to no avail. The model T, loaded to the gills, kept gaining speed and barely made it around some of the hairpin turns in the road. Finally, on a steep decline, Oscar decided they couldn't make the next turn and he told Noan to jump. The truck hit a bump on the side of the road and started over the hillside. Next thing Noan knew, she was lying flat on her back halfway down the hill and there was the truck above her just tipping over and about to roll down on top of her. Oscar had jumped and was hanging from a tree limb above her.

When rescuers found them, Noan was still lying on the ground. The truck had somehow miraculously bounced over her, only hitting her foot and breaking it. Oscar was walking around just fine and dandy. Somehow they managed to save the Model T and the furniture. In the days of the depression you managed to save everything.

Elsie and Oscar's family car was an old Hudson Touring Sedan. It had a self starter which, of course, didn't always work. So you had to crank that huge engine by hand to get it started and it didn't like to start at all. One day the generator gave up completely and Oscar decided to go see Dan Cohen who ran a junk yard. Cohen had a bunch of old junkers parked in the back of his yard, and Oscar decided there must be an old Hudson back in there that might just have a generator in some sort of working order. Well, Dan told him to go back and look and see if he could find one. Oscar lucked out and found one that looked pretty good, so he disconnected it with his own tools, took it up to Dan and said he wanted to check it out to see if it fit his Hudson. Dan told him to go ahead. So Oscar went across the street and proceeded to install it in his old Hudson and it worked fine. Then Oscar took the bad generator back and told Dan it didn't fit, sorry. Dan said, "OK, sorry you couldn't find one". And away Oscar went with his new working generator and the money for a new one still in his pocket. As I said, Oscar didn't mind cutting corners.

The most important of the three Zeiler sisters to me, of course, was my mother, Lenore. She was born in Alma, Wisconsin, on June 14, 1893, the youngest of the three girls and the prettiest - and was completely spoiled by her parents. She was baptized "Lanor Prudence Zeiler." Once she was old enough she changed the spelling to "Lenore,", later for a short time to "Lenoir," and when she was much older back to "Lanor." It depended on her mood of the moment, I suppose. Her father called her "Nony." That was too long a name for me, so I shortened it to Noan. I never referred to her as "mom," "mama," or "mother." I don't know why. She was always just Noan from the time I was a little boy. Perhaps it was for the same reason I called my father "LB" on occasion, although most of the time he was "Pop."
After Noan married LB, he continued to spoil her like her parents had, and it seemed she always got her way. She came to California in 1916 with Augie and Emily, which, incidentally, is what I called my grandparents—never "grandma" or "grandpa." The three of them moved from Alma to 1200 Lincoln Avenue in St Paul, Minnesota and then they came to California, folowing Noan's older sisters Elsie and Adeline ("Bebe"). They migrated to California a few years earlier and were painting a glorious picture of life in San Francisco. LB was working for the San Francisco Junior Chamber of Commerce when Noan met him. I don't think they went together long before they got married. Noan was a very pretty young girl. Once they were married LB moved in with Augie and Emily in the big flat on Potrero and 21st street, and it was there that I was born. I still have vague memories of that place and walking through the gardens of the catholic hospital across the

street with my mother and grandmother. We weren't there too many years when LB went into the real estate business with a man named Dave Black and we moved to the apartment house on Taylor and Washington on Nob Hill. Augie and Em went with us and we lived there until about 1927 when we moved to the "Big House" in Almaden.

The Big House is now known as the "Casa Grande," and was originally built in 1852 to house the management of the New Almaden Quicksilver Mine. It is currently a county park and home to a museum. By 1927 the mine was closed and Dave Black owned a lot of the property in the area. He hired my father to sell real estate and offered to let us live in the Big House. It had almost thirty bedrooms and a kitchen the size of some homes. What an experience that was for a little kid who had been cooped up in an apartment or flat all of his life in San Francisco! I truly loved Almaden. There were 15 acres or more of grounds around the Big House, most of it landscaped, with a 300-foot pool in back for swimming. In the middle of the pool was a small island and there were row-boats for leisurely trips about the "lake."

Noan started me in grammar school shortly after we moved down to Almaden. The school house, which only contained the first three grades, was located just about a half mile from our house, so I walked to school every morning. During my "early" years, Noan had read to me often and taught me how to recognize the alphabet and read words, so when I got into grammar school, I was a whiz! Noan suddenly decided I was too smart for my class, so she convinced the teachers to promote me in what was about half the time. During those years I had the pleasure of attending this quaint little country school. It had a creek running through the property where we could go and play during recess.

One Christmas we made little Santa dolls with the legs and

arms which moved when you pulled on strings. I told Noan that I had a lot of crayon work to do on it, so she took me down to the school house on a Saturday. No one was around, but, of course, the schoolrooms were locked. So we went around to the back door of my classroom and found the door held shut with only a hook and eye. She found some kind of a stick that she could stick through the crack and unhook the door and we went in and I

A Lenore (aka Nony) Wilson Beginner's Dictionary

Noan had a vocabulary all her own, and I'm sorry I didn't keep track of it earlier, since I believe I have forgotten much of it. Many of these had their roots in German, which she spoke well enough to converse with Bebe or Emily when she didn't want me to understand what she was saying. Some that come to mind are **"rootch, potchie, fid, dreep soller, cripfy drik"** as in: "He went down the *rootch* on his *fid*, and scratched his *potchie* and walked away like a *cripfy drik*. But he was no *dreep soller*." So what does all that mean?

Well, a "*rootch*" can be a verb or a noun, depending. It is a slide, usually somewhat rough, where you slide your bottom voluntarily or with the help of gravity. As a verb, you can "*rootch*" down the hill to the bottom. A "*fid*" is your rear end, sometimes called a "*French fid*" when it is all washed and powdered! A "*potchie*" is usually the palm of your hand, or in the case of a small child, the whole hand. A "*cripfy drik*" is someone who moves rather slowly, may be stooped somewhat. And a "*dreep soller*" is someone who complains a lot, is never happy, and maybe cries a lot.

The most famous rootch that I can remember was in Reeve's Canyon. Here are a few expressions from Nony spelled phonetically :

Boomel: To waste away, like. "He sure boomels his money."
Con-ima-widely-lowfa: He, she, it – can hardly walk.
Cripfy Drik: A stooped, slow-moving or tired, worn-out person.
Drellily: (making a d....) when you let your lower lip hang down, when you are kind of sad.
Dreep-soller: A person who complains a lot, is never happy, and cries a lot.
Doichee-nunder: A terrible mess. (As on your desk top, or in your whole house).
Fid: Your bottom. **French Fid:** A nice clean powdered bottom.
Goorpse: A light belch
Loosh: To have a desire for something, like: I have a loosh for a banana split.
Lootch: To suck on something like hard candy, etc.
Kootchie: A tickly feeling in your chest caused by excitement and sheer happiness.
Potchie: (Or "Patchie") Your hands or palms.
Rootch: A slide or place in dirt where you can slide.
Shtoortz: When you are so excited you are about to have a hemmhorage, you are about to have a shtoortz.
Verbutz: When you can't "verbutz" something, you can't stand it.
Wezza: A celebration or party. When you "make a wezza" about something, you make a big fuss! A "Family Wezza" is the best kind.

proceeded to color my doll. How many mothers aid you with breaking and entering?

One winter day I was very sick and unable to go to school. Noan held my head in her lap as we sat on the couch in the sun at the end of the big old dining room and she read to me from my school books so that I wouldn't miss anything. It was such a pleasant experience, even though I wasn't feeling well at all. I hated to miss school. I always thought I'd miss something important!

I got through the first three grades in a year and a half, and skipped the fourth grade completely. The next school house, which housed the 4th and 5th grades, was about 5 miles down the road and I had to take the bus. Noan somehow believed in a hot lunch the year 'round. So she drove down to the school house at lunch time every day and brought me my lunch. Then we would drive down the road to some picturesque place and park and I would eat my lunch. This continued all the way through the 5th grade. It wasn't until late in the sixth grade that I finally got to eat lunch in the school cafeteria or carry my lunch - whichever we could afford. Near the end of the 5th grade, the old school house was closed, along with the two that housed the other grades, and we were moved into a beautiful brand new school house that housed all eight grades. It may have been considered progress, but I missed those old schoolhouses.

The last thing I remember about the 5th grade school was one late afternoon when we were all out waiting for the school bus to come and pick us up. Some of the mean kids who were always up to some deviltry had found a nail. When there was no traffic in sight they ran out into the middle of the road, set the nail up on its head, and ran back. A car came by and the nail was now lying on its side. So, they'd try it again. Many times it just fell over. Finally, I said (smart ass kid that I was), "You're doing it all wrong...here, let me show you." I skittered out, lined up the nail with the tire tracks, and carefully propped it up with pebbles. Then we waited a while for a car to show up. Pretty soon a big old Cadillac came by driven by a huge woman. After she whizzed by, we went out to look. The pebbles were scattered a bit and the nail was gone! "Ooooh!" the mean kids said, "You're gonna get it now!" (As though it wasn't their idea all along! I was just the kid who was smart enough to make it work.) I didn't confess when I got home (I was too smart for that too) but I always felt bad about it. In 1920s rural Almaden there was no convenient Emergency Road Service!

Noan would often tell me about her childhood in Alma, Wisconsin. That's when I first learned about the exploits of her friends George Shetley and Hunzy Bourkharte, and of her trips up to her Aunt Mary's farm. She and some of the kids once found a dead cow lying on its side just below a small bluff. Someone thought it would be fun to get up on the bluff and jump off onto the dead cow, which was well bloated by this time. So, they did, and I wish I could say it exploded on one of the jumps, but it appeared to hold up quite well! Finally her Uncle found out what they were doing and ended the fun.

Another time Noan was crossing a pasture that she was supposed to stay out of, since there was a mean bull grazing there. Well, of course, the bull saw her and started to charge. She ran like crazy and managed to get to the gate about the same time as the bull. She went over the gate and sprawled on the other side. Meanwhile, her Uncle saw what was going on and came running to protect her with the only thing he had - a sledge hammer! He went through the gate and started cussing out that bull and then to emphasize his remarks, he whopped that old bull right between the eyes with the sledge hammer, hard enough to stagger him. To both

Noan's and her Uncle's relief everyone turned out fine, including the bull.

One weekend the local Holy Baptists organized a big baptismal event in the Mississippi for that Sunday. The day before they put some stakes and ribbons in the water to show where the shallow shelf ended. That night Noan's friends George and Hunzy pulled up the stakes and moved them out a few feet. The next morning the minister and the poor baptizee were seen dropping out of sight when they went off the shelf into the deep Mississippi. No one knew who did it, but I think they suspected!

My father, Lee Bradford Wilson, was born in Fayetteville, Ohio, on April 3, 1890, and everyone called him "LB.". He was the third son of Tom Wilson and Narissa Christiancy Wilson. It is very hard to think of Grandma Wilson as a young girl. She looked very old from the first time I saw her. She had grey hair which was done up in a bun on top of her head, lots of wrinkles, and a thin face that wasn't inclined to smile much. I don't know much about her life while LB was growing up, but I suspect it wasn't all that easy. She was left at an early age with three young boys. Her husband Tom, who worked as a barber in Fayetteville, died when LB was only two years old. Her oldest boy, George only lived about eight years longer and passed away. That left Ross, the middle boy, and LB. At some point in time they moved to Ann Arbor, Michigan. LB completed High School there and went to Michigan State University for a year or two and then in 1908 or 1909 he decided he was going to go to California to make his fame and fortune. I don't know how the separation went, whether he had his mother's blessing or not, but he packed his things and together with a buddy he rode the rails on freight trains all the way to San Francisco. Seems that was a common practice in those days.

I was never made aware of what transpired during the years between his arrival in San Francisco and meeting my mother in 1919. He was 27 at the time of World War I, just a few years too old to be drafted. Evidently he felt no compunction to join up. Ross, however, enlisted early and went to France where he was wounded and sent to a hospital in Ireland to recover. There he met and fell in love with Martha, a nurse in his hospital, whom he married and brought home with him.

Ross was a very kind and gentle man. I never ever heard him raise his voice or get agitated over anything. But then that was true of LB, also. Sometime in the late twenties, just before the onslaught of the depression, Ross and Martha adopted Martha's sister's girl Jeanie who was living at home with her family in Ireland. The family had too many children to support and Ross and Martha, who were childless, wanted to help out. So they had Jeanie, who was only 5 at the time, sent over here on a passenger ship, then by train from New York to Oakland, California, all alone. Ross worked in Berkeley as a Landscape Gardener for some of the wealthier people of the area and did all right for himself. I can remember the very first time they brought Jeanie down to see us in Almaden. She was such a tiny tot and spoke with a thick Irish brogue!

During the Almaden years, we went up to visit Ross and family in Berkeley often. Grandma Wilson was living with them and she was always so glad to see her youngest son. He seemed to be her favorite - I don't know why. No one could have treated her any better than Ross. If she ever had any misgivings about LB's leaving home and coming to California, all was forgiven.

LB was always a strong believer in exercise and Almaden was his cup of tea. We had acres of lawn all around the place and he would thoroughly enjoy getting out there with a push-me lawn mower, mowing that lawn in the early morning. When we first arrived there was a full-time gardener who took care of all the shrubs and trees and watered everything, but as the depression took hold, that was a luxury they couldn't afford, so we did everything.

My dad still had high hopes that real estate would pick up and he had Elmer build a small stand across Almaden Road from the Big House where, with banners flying, it was announced that they had beautiful weekend homes for sale, vacation homes, and summer homes. This was at a time when most people couldn't afford one home. Dave Black even invested in building a "spec" house on the back road. It was a really nice place. But as far as I could remember, that house was still for sale when we all moved away years later.

Being in real estate, LB worked seven days a week although he often came home early on Saturday and only worked half a day on Sundays. Summers were a great time. As soon as he got home, he'd get into his swimming trunks and we'd hot foot it down the road to the old swimming hole. He loved swimming. In fact, I remember one winter in Almaden, determined not to let the weather deter him, he jumped off the spring board into the big pool and broke the thin layer of ice on the surface with his head. He was such a Pa! Noan and I had to work on him, but we'd almost always get him to go to the "movie of the week" on Sunday nights in Ukiah. We didn't take vacations of any duration, but occasionally we would go down to San Francisco, stay at the Golden State or the Manx Hotel, go to movies, eat at fancy restaurants - all in a single weekend. This usually happened when LB had a client to see. So he would go take care of business while Noan and I went shopping. Then we'd meet back at the hotel about 5 p.m. I didn't mind going shopping with Noan - I'd been doing it since I was 4 years old. I was always dressed in a suit and tie and I'd go in the big Emporium and stand near the front counters and frequently people would come up to me to ask me directions, taking me for a floor walker. I got a kick out of that.

    This was the depression era and no one had any money. Of course, the real estate business fell apart completely and since that was the reason we had moved to Almaden something else had to take its place. Well, Dave Black, who owned Almaden together with his brothers Ben and Zizz, decided he could turn it into a recreational park. They had these beautiful spacious lawns, the huge pool, and they put in an outdoor dance floor. A three to five piece band was hired to play on Saturday nights. I used to stand next to the piano player and I noticed that every time they'd start a new tune, he would stamp his foot three times. So, after a while I started stamping my foot just before he did and this disconcerted him no end. He finally asked me to move away.
    The Katz family - Elmer Katz, his wife and his two sons, Niles and Herbert - lived on the other side of the creek from the Big House. Herbert was in the same class in grammar school that I was, except he was probably three or four years older. He got into the fifth grade and couldn't seem to get his knees under the desk anymore, so he quit school and went to work with his father, along with Niles. Elmer was sort of a handyman around Almaden, taking on big and small projects So, when the County mandated that if we wanted to open our beautiful pool to public swimming, we would have to build vertical walls and make it up to eight feet deep, Elmer volunteered to do the job. And what a job that was! This was a 300-foot pool, free form, with a small Island in the middle of the shallow end. They decided to bisect the pool at the widest and deepest end, run the vertical walls across the free form pool which would essentially turn the "lake" into three separate

pools, with the public swimming at one end in the deep pool. The upper end was the smallest and shallowest and could be turned into a kiddies' swimming pool. The largest end contained the island and a beautiful fountain and would remain relatively untouched. It looked weird with those vertical walls sticking up out of the shallow pool on the lower end. Elmer built the forms, put in horizontal re-bars, and mixed concrete with a little old putzy-putzy two stroke mixer. All the sand and gravel had to be shoveled into the mixer by Herb and Niles.

About this time - for some reason lost in the antiquities of time - Noan went to visit Elsie in Redwood Valley. It must have been during the school season, since I didn't go. Elmer finished the pouring and took off the forms. The next Saturday they started to fill the deep pool. My pop and I were asleep in the big upstairs bedroom that night when we heard this tremendous roar. He put some clothes on and went down to investigate. When he got back he just said, "The wall broke." The next morning I went down to look it over and there were huge chunks of concrete way up on the far end of that 300 foot pool. The break took out the whole center section of the new vertical wall, including the horizontal re-bar. Elmer took it in his stride. Even Dave Black, who was footing the bill, didn't get too upset. Instead, they just went back to the task of cleaning it all up and starting over. And you can't say that Elmer didn't learn from his mistakes. He not only laced together vertical and horizontal re-bar, but he built in buttresses that raised from the floor of the long shallow pool up to the top of the wall at a 45 degree angle. In addition, he doubled the thickness of the wall. He wasn't going to have it fall a second time. In those depression era times, you hired handymen to do your construction jobs. Licensed contractors were too expensive. Obviously, Elmer was not a contractor.

That same winter we had a doozy of a storm. Almaden was in a narrow canyon and heavy rains made the creek rise. At the upper end of the canyon was a lake over a half mile long and well over a ¼ mile wide called "Lake Almaden." This lake was formed at the "Dump" where the retorts for the quicksilver mines were operated. Over the years, a huge pit developed that eventually was closed off with an earthen dam. This, as it filled up, it became Lake Almaden. It wasn't used for anything. The land around it was mostly red cinnabar, well ground up and not conducive to growing much of anything. This winter Lake Almaden was at last doomed. Behind the big house and over a small hill ran the creek. The hill kept the creek in its channel. Crossing the creek at this point was a footbridge suspended by cables that I used to love to run across. It felt "keen" as we said in those days, to feel it swing underfoot as you crossed it. On the other side it met a path that ran up to Maggie Lawler's house. Maggie was an old spinster who lived there alone and had us over to dinner every now and then. She, along with quite a few other people, had houses there on the "Back Road," and the bridge was built to accommodate people who wanted to get from one road to the other without having to hike up to the head of the canyon and take the road bridge. It was the only access to the back road until that night. I don't know how long it rained, but we had more than our share. Sometime in the middle of the night, another roar came. This time, the earthen dam gave way and the whole lake came roaring down the canyon, sweeping out the cabled bridge and anything else that stood in its way. Fortunately, it stayed on the creek side of the hill. Otherwise, it would have filled up our beautiful pond with mud and sludge.

One night I got in trouble with Elmer Katz and a Ouija board. Elmer and his wife and his two boys came over for dinner. My folks talked themselves out and were groping for a new subject when Noan got off on one of her tangents about mystical things and that lead around to Ouija boards. I was just a kid, but I figured out that they had to be as phony as a three dollar bill. Noan got out her Ouija board and she and Elmer sat there concentrating on a question one of them had asked it. Well, their hands were tiring as they had them suspended over the pointer with their fingers barely touching it. Finally, I think one of them got the palsy or something and their hands kind of got an ever so slight tremor in them which were transferred to the pointer. It didn't seem to go anywhere important, but if you wait long enough it will eventually get to a letter of the alphabet or the "yes and no" boxes. However, either they weren't actually helping it along or the "Ouija" was asleep, because it never spelled out a satisfactory answer. After a while I said, "Let me try." I took Noan's place. Noan told Elmer to ask a question. He said, "All right. Where is my mother?" Well, I took a look at Elmer and he looked pretty old to me - after all, I was just a kid. So, I thought, this was a trick question by Elmer - she must be dead. So very subtly I dropped my right thumb nail just below the edge of the pointer. This allowed the participant to gently move the pointer any direction without pushing it so hard that the other person will feel the push. Gradually, I spelled out "She's dead." Well, Elmer's rugged complexion turned two shades whiter. He was BUYING this whole thing and, presumably, she had been alive up to the point that I decided to bury her with the Ouija board! Being a stubborn kid, I decided I had to be right, so I continued writing—"died recently." Well, Noan couldn't take any more of that, as Elmer said, "She's alive and well living in Oklahoma, I believe". Noan said, "Of course she is, you can't believe everything this thing says." A few minutes before she had been praising the Ouija as the great Oracle!! And she gave me a look that would roast chestnuts without an open fire!! The Katzes left for home shortly thereafter with Elmer saying he thought he'd call home to Oklahoma to see how his mother was doing. After they were gone, my mother gave me a stern loud lecture on "manipulating the Ouija" while my father sat in an easy chair reading the Saturday Evening Post. I seem to remember him having the trace of smile on his face.

I loved the fall of the year in Almaden when the many tall sycamores lost their leaves. We would rake them all together burn the piles. It smelled so good. And when I got a pile of leaves really big, I would jump in them before I burned them.

The walkway underneath the dance floor was poured concrete which Elmer marked off in squares and then divided the squares diagonally. Each triangle he sprinkled with a different colored powder which was then trowled into the concrete. It made a rather attractive cheap walk, but the color bleached out after a year or so. Along the walkway they set up a snack stand where we served hot dogs, ice cream, soft drinks, candy bars, and gum. I worked behind the counter often during the summer. Eventually I ordered the soft drinks from the NEHI distributor that came around each week. In those days, Coca Cola was a new beverage, and although we carried it, NEHI was the most popular and came in over a half-dozen flavors. I ordered the ice cream from the Golden State dairy truck that came by. I thought I was quite the businessman!

The recreational park went pretty well, and LB was put in charge as general manager. Unfortunately it wasn't extremely profitable, at least for LB. Noan, in order to make ends meet, went to work 5 days a week for a wholesale candy house in San Jose. She made the magnificent sum of $2 a day –or $10 a week. From this, she bought gasoline, food, and paid to have the small house built in Redwood Valley for Augie and Em to live in. I don't know how

Noan managed all of that on $10 a week, but she did. I would shop for groceries with her and it was sort of like a game, seeing how much food you could get for the lowest price. We would come out of that grocery store with an entire basketful of groceries for only $2. You could get a loaf of bread for 5 cents. Gasoline, during some of the frequent price wars, was just a nickel a gallon - and that was full service! Noan continued working at the wholesale house until we moved to Redwood Valley in 1934.

Things finally got so tight financially that Noan and I moved up to Redwood Valley to live with my Aunt Bebe and her husband Nate. LB stayed in Almaden for another year. I think he was afraid to take a chance on moving up there. But things only got worse in Almaden and he finally chucked it all and came up and joined us in 1935. It was a good move. The depression wasn't over, but it was improving slightly and he was invited to join Bill Hagan, an insurance man, in his Ukiah office. Things started going pretty well after that. During the first year up there, Noan got a job with the District Attorney's Office which helped out a lot. After LB got going with Bill Hagan, Noan quit working and she stayed home forevermore. I started high school and Noan saw me growing up - something she really didn't want to see happen. As a result we had some very strong arguments from time to time. My problem was that I always answered her back—and that got me nowhere. Whenever she argued with LB, it was strictly one-sided. He wouldn't argue with her and generally it all blew over faster than my arguments!

Actually, the move to Redwood Valley had another fortunate side effect. During all those years in the Big House in Almaden I never got really close to my father. Although he was always there, it seemed as though all of his time was taken up by one thing or another. Even in my young mind, the uncertainty of making a living bothered me. We never talked about it, but it was ever present. In Ukiah, my father had a job he went to every day, but he came home at night and he was all mine and in our own home. He also became a different man. I'm sure he was bothered all those years by the uncertainties of the future and with each passing year things got better. First, we added a small addition to the kitchen, put in running water and toilet and bath. Then a short time later, in what became an obsession with Noan, we built on a much larger addition to the kitchen, a separate bedroom for me, and a much enlarged living room. Things were definitely getting better!

I graduated from High School in 1938 and I think it was Noan's intention to keep me living at home forever. I had no car and no job, which was fine with her. She paid for music lessons and I studied the piano for a year. I was not born to play the piano. My hands weren't synchronized. Soon after that first year, we joined the Ukiah Community Players, together with my cousin Virginia and her husband Curtis. The players decided to put on a show for the "men in the service" who were the first draftees of the pre-war era. There was a small army base in Willits and we scheduled a show for them. Well, I was the only one who volunteered to write the show, so I did the deed. After several weeks of rehearsing, we put the show on, along with a few mistakes - like the gun didn't go off when Curtis was supposed to be shot. I quickly adlibbed, "He's shot! And the gunman used a silencer, too!!" Curtis didn't hear my line and started to get back up. I couldn't have that, so I put my foot on his head and held him down. I have no idea how all this looked to the service men, but they seemed to enjoy it. We had such a good time putting that show on that I wrote & made a silent 8mm black and white movie titled "Murder on Bare Mountain" using the same cast.

Noan took part in all these activities, but after the movie was over there wasn't much looming ahead to interest me. The war was on the horizon - we all knew it - and sooner or later I'd have to join the Army. I couldn't bear to tell Noan this - I knew she'd have a fit. Those summers I worked for Uncle Oscar, harvesting the grapes and saving what little money I earned for whatever the future held.

This, then, is the family and the background I came from. I considered myself a pretty average, everyday young guy. And soon I, like many of the other "average, everyday young guys" across America, would be thrust into extraordinary circumstances.

2

December 7, 1941
The War arrives in America

By the end of 1941 Japan had grown tired of waiting for a good reason to destroy our Pacific fleet, so they just went ahead and did it. Or at least they made a good try. You can take a ferry out to the Arizona Memorial in Pearl Harbor and look down through the crystal clear waters and see the giant battleship Arizona lying at the bottom. Many other ships were sunk along with the Arizona. Our Pacific fleet took a tremendous beating on that date. But, unfortunately for the Japanese, our aircraft carriers were out on maneuvers. Up until December 6, there had been a number of isolationists in this country, mostly politicians, who kept saying that what happened in Europe was none of our business. After all, that was three thousand miles away and we were perfectly safe, surrounded by two oceans and protected by our fleet. Most of us knew that the day we would enter the war would arrive sooner or later, although not in the way that it did. It was just a matter of time until America would join the allies, regardless of what the isolationists said. And on the day that war was declared the isolationists disappeared and America was united in one goal - complete and total victory. So, strange as it seemed to us even at the time, America's participation in the European war was sparked by an attack from Japan.

    I was putting a coat of shellac on the hall floor on the morning that we heard the news. Of course, there was no television in those days, so our news came over the radio. We did not have our radio on that day and we got a call from my Aunt Bebe who lived about a mile away. She said, "The Japs have bombed Honolulu! Turn on your radio!" We turned it on and sat there glued to the announcer's voice as he reiterated over and over again the only news he had so far. My shellac dried quickly and I still sat there transfixed by this news with only half of the hallway finished. My mother cried, as you might expect. My father looked rather grim but didn't have much to say except to console my mother. The news was all bad. Our fleet was destroyed. There was no mention yet that our aircraft carriers that had been out at sea and missed being sunk by the dive bombers.

Every day we kept our radios from dawn to dusk, tuned in to every newscast. On Monday, President Franklin Delano Roosevelt gave a very serious address to both houses of Congress and they promptly declared war on Japan. Hitler, meanwhile, had decided that Japan would destroy the military might - what there was of it - of the United States, and he didn't want to be left out of the victory that was to come, so he promptly declared war on the United States. Now his subs could sink everything in the Atlantic Ocean that sailed to Britain. He was jubilant. So Congress returned the favor and declared war on Germany as well. It had truly became a "World War."

In our family we talked about the war a lot, and would gladly have done away with Hitler if we could get a hold of him. But we never discussed my personal entry into the conflict. My parents, of course, had lived through the first World War, the war that made the world safe for democracy, and I don't think they wanted to consider the thought that they would have to send off their only son off to fight yet another war just 21 years after the last one had ended. My father was a quiet man and seldom offered his opinion on anything. If asked he would offer what sounded to me at least, a reasonably sound, logical reply. He was a staunch Republican and Franklin Delano Roosevelt was President. As a result, he could say nothing very favorable about the President. I called myself a Republican as well, but I admired Roosevelt and secretly agreed with him on many of his programs, a feeling that would eventually lead me to become a Democrat. William Randolph Hearst ran the newspaper world at that time and, of course, was also a strong Republican. My father lived and breathed the San Francisco Examiner, and everything that Hearst said had to be right. Later in the war Hearst got into trouble when he published an editorial cartoon. This was right after Hitler invaded Russia and now Russia became our ally. Naturally, Hearst was against Communism as much as National Socialism, so he had a hard time accepting Stalin as an ally. The cartoon showed two snakes labeled Hitler and Stalin devouring each other. The caption read, "Let's hope the consummation is complete." As a new ally, the government did not take kindly to this at all. Well, I thought, these are confusing times. It's hard to tell who your friends are.

Those of us who lived in California felt like we were living on the front line. The Japanese hadn't hesitated to bomb Hawaii, Guam, Midway, or any other US possession in the Pacific. When would they decide to bomb - or even invade - California? And, of course, during those early months, the news was all bad. The Japanese had sunk The Prince of Wales, Britain's largest battleship, and were in the process of taking all of Southeast Asia. The Philippines were under attack with General Douglas MacArthur retreating onto the Bataan Peninsula. It didn't make us feel a whole lot better when he was removed by submarine and sent to Australia. We were retreating! That wasn't the American way! We always fought and won our battles. But it would be some time until we started to make any progress, and then it would happen in North Africa, not the Pacific.

America's army consisted of young civilians spread across the nation from every walk of life, many who had never fired a weapon of any kind. I had a .22 caliber hunting rifle with which I had hunted rabbits and that was the sum total of my knowledge about weapons. I was 20 at the time of Pearl Harbor and wanted to enlist, but which branch? I thought the Navy looked pretty keen, but when they sunk those battleships, there was an awful lot of deep water around that did not seem too attractive. Being in The Army meant you would be digging fox holes and getting caught in the gun sights of every German soldier in Europe. So that left the Army Air Force. That sounded pretty attractive. You were up above the ground action, you had control of your destiny, I thought—since you were flying the plane. Naturally, all of us who joined the AAF were determined to pilot P-38's or P-51's. I didn't know anyone who thought of flying bombers. We pictured ourselves strafing trains, shooting down enemy fighters, dropping an occasional single bomb into a train tunnel - in other words, destroying the enemy almost single handedly.

As soon as war was declared, I had to register with selective service and wait to be called up for training. In June, 1942, the local draft board said I would be called up within the next two weeks. I didn't want the ground Army; I wanted the Air Force. So my mother took me down to San Francisco where I went to the Air Force recruiting office and signed up for Aviation Cadet Training.

I remember giving the recruitment officer my information.

"Your name?" he asked.

"Bradford Perry Wilson," I responded.

"Your home?"

"Redwood Valley."

"Where is that?"

"Just eight miles north of Ukiah."

"Ukiah—where's that?"

"About 125 miles north of San Francisco, on the Redwood Highway."

Ukiah - he didn't even know where it was?! I had visited my Aunt Elsie and Uncle Oscar on their ranch in Redwood Valley many summers as a young boy and I loved those weekly trips we made to Ukiah to shop. It was just a small town at that time, about 3000 people. The main north-south highway, US 101, went right through the middle of town, and the traffic was so light in the late 1920's that when they had a carnival come to town, they would close the main street and set up the carnival right on the street in front of the county courthouse. By the time I moved up to Redwood Valley, in 1934, the town had grown considerably and the carnivals were set up on fields north of town. That year I enrolled in high school in Ukiah and rode the bus in each morning.

Our home was situated on a small bluff above US 101 right at a junction with a county road. It had been built in the early 1930's. We moved in shortly after I started going to high school. The house was gradually enlarged. My mother loved to "make changes." First a bedroom was added for me with a hallway alongside leading to the front door. Then the kitchen was remodeled, but that was only temporary until Noan decided it still had to be bigger, and we doubled the size. My pop went along with these changes stoically. Very few people hired contractors for that kind of work. We hired a carpenter and I learned a lot about building from him, knowledge that I would put to good use after the war when my wife and I built our own home with no outside help. My father just wasn't a do-it-yourself-er. So I did all the "constructing" that wasn't done by the carpenter.

There were no nearby neighbors. At first just the three of us lived there along with Rowdy, a stray cat who had adopted us. Pop loved cats. He liked to carry Rowdy draped across the back of his neck with his feet hanging down on each side. Later, in early 1936, Snuffy, our big ol' dog adopted us, too. He was wandering along the highway one day probably having fallen out of a car or truck, howling in loneliness, and Noan heard him. She called to him, he came bounding up the bluff and then stayed for fourteen years! He and Rowdy got along better than any cat and dog I've ever known. Maybe they knew they were two lost souls who had found the right home and had better stick together.

Although it was now growing quite rapidly, Ukiah still had the small town atmosphere. There were two chain grocery stores in town, Safeway and Purity, which started out with small stores where every customer was waited on individually, with every grocery selection being obtained by the clerk from very high shelves behind the counter. The era of self-service shopping had not yet reached Ukiah. There were a number of small independent groceries doing business the same way. The State Theater on North State Street showed all the movies. The really big movies were scheduled for Sunday and Monday, a minor movie on Tuesday, an "almost" big movie on Wednesday and Thursday, and a double feature (with at least one of them being a western) on Friday and Saturday. If a really, *really* big movie came along, it might even play Sunday through Tuesday. And, so we got to see just about everything Hollywood provided.

There were, at one time, three weekly newspapers in town to provide all the news you could possibly want to hear. There was one small grocery store run by a man named Jack Gooch, where my aunt could bring in her fresh-from-the-nest eggs, and trade them for her other grocery needs. There were many Native Americans living on nearby Rancherias, and they always came to Ukiah on Saturday to shop and spend a few hours sitting on the park benches outside the County Courthouse, enjoying the sights of the "big city". Ukiah was a typical small town of that era, but showing dangerous signs of growing. And the end of the war would accelerate that growth beyond my wildest imagination.

As I've described, we lived in a rural area whose mailing address was "Redwood Valley," but actually the village itself that was composed of two buildings; a general store and post office. They were about two miles from our house on the county road—not in the direction of Ukiah. Therefore, we didn't visit it very often. When we needed something from the store and didn't want to go all the way into Ukiah, we would drive south on US 101 about two miles to Calpella, another little village that consisted of a general store, a post office, *and* two gas stations.

The Calpella general store should have been preserved as a national shrine to all general stores in the small towns of this nation. The roof extended out over the driveway and included two gas pumps at the roadside, pumps with big handles on the side with which the proprietor would pump the gas up into a ten gallon glass tank at the top. Then he would give you whatever amount of gas you wanted—up to 10 gallons. If you wanted more, he'd have to pump it up again, run it into your tank till it was full, and then deduct the amount left in the glass tank. This procedure was not too exacting.

A large porch contained several newspaper racks for the "big city" newspapers, and an ice cream counter where the owner dished up the best cones in the state. The store had a big squeaky screen door that was pulled shut by a spring and slammed on your heels if you didn't watch it. Inside, there was a candy counter offering chocolate creams and other assorted delights, followed by a fresh meat counter, the grocery shelves, and assorted pickle barrels and cracker barrels. On the left were islands piled with clothing, featuring Levi's Jeans, assorted hats, shirts, shoes and boots, and just about everything you could possibly need—if you worked on a ranch. The whole store smelled delicious, as the scents of all these things blended together. It was a Sunday ritual in the early 1930's for Aunt Elsie to take me down to Calpella and get the Sunday paper and a vanilla ice cream cone. It was a very sad day in the late 30's when the store burned to the ground and was never replaced.

Now that I had enlisted I knew that I wouldn't be drafted. Instead I now had to suffer the waiting game of when I might be called up. They said it might take a while before the training bases were built and staffed. America was definitely not prepared to go to war.

It turned out to be more than six months before they called me, and since I never knew when the call would come, I couldn't do much. I couldn't start college or accept a full-time job. All that time I was chafing at the bit, oh, so eager to get at those Nazis and the Japanese Empire. It's surprising now, looking back from the cusp of the twenty-first century, to realize I never met a single soldier during World War II who wasn't ready, willing, and eager to get into the fracas! An enemy had dared to attack us! The American culture at the time still held by the code of the old west, and we were determined to retaliate.

So I spent those months going to the movies, and when it got warm many afternoons at my favorite swimming hole. Over the summer and early fall we spent several weekends up in Reeves Canyon camping. When December came, my dog Snuffy and I went up to the "Flat" and got a Christmas tree. We shopped for

Christmas and did all the usual things. Finally on December 12th - just barely more than a year after Pearl Harbor - I got a letter from the USAAF telling me I was to report to Santa Ana Army Air Base on Monday, December 14th, 1942.   That was just two days, and Redwood Valley was a long ways from Santa Ana! That put a rush on our Christmas plans.

My father, LB, as a real estate broker, had benefited from the growth of the town over the past eight years. The only problem with selling real estate was that it was a seven day a week job. There was never a day when he didn't go into the office to take some clients out and show them ranches, timber, and other properties. I wondered what the war would do to the real estate business. I needn't have worried—it went on as usual. When my pop got home that night he was cheerful and not openly concerned about my finally having received my notice to report for duty. Whatever deep feelings he had about my going into action, he didn't reveal them until much later.

When Noan saw my letter, she was, of course, as most mothers were when their sons were going off to war - very upset. I knew better than to give her an extra hug or unusual display of emotion that evening - any deviation from normality and she would burst into tears. She was an emotional person.

Since it was just 12 days before Christmas, we had finished our Christmas shopping, and we were planning the usual family Christmas at our house. This was a Saturday afternoon and I would have to leave at 4am Sunday morning. We had twelve hours to get the family together and celebrate Christmas early. So our Christmas came on December 12th that year. We all got together on very short notice; my aunt Bebe, and Uncle Nate, my cousin Virginia and her husband Curtis, and my grandmother, Emily. We had our somewhat abbreviated Christmas meal, and opened all of our presents. I have no memory of what I got that Christmas. What do you give a young man who is leaving for the service? There's not much he can take with him, but I know I opened a bunch of presents. My dear Emily was holding up quite well. We had celebrated her 87th birthday the previous June and she was still strong and in good health. We were very close and I was afraid that my leaving would be bad for her. But she just "knew" that I was going to be all right and that I'd come home after the war. And she went home that night with lots of hugs and kisses and no tears. Virginia and Curtis were about 10 years older than I, but they were the closest thing I had to a brother or a sister. They lived on the ranch that had belonged to Virginia's parents (Oscar and Elsie, who, had driven themselves to early deaths working on their ranch.) Curtis had enrolled in the draft but hadn't been called as yet. He became a casualty of the war in a different way. He and Virginia were divorced when he returned. I seldom saw him after that. Bebe, Noan's eldest sister, and her husband Nate lived less than a mile from Noan and Pop. Noan spent much time with Bebe, and I was glad for that. I would be missed more if she were alone all day.

The three of us, Noan, pop, and I, stayed up the rest of the night, since we had to leave for the train station at 3:30. There was no discussion about the war or what I would be doing. Noan was tense, but she didn't show any other emotion and if my dad was tense, he didn't show it at all.

Pop was such an easy going guy. He never got into an argument with my mother, although she would have a one-sided argument with him that would sometimes last for hours. He'd just be quiet and that infuriated her, no end! Every night all summer when he got home from the office, he would put on his swim shorts and run down to the old swimming hole for an early evening swim. When he came back up, he would take a cocktail out in the patio, and sit on a chaise and read the Saturday Evening Post or the San Francisco Examiner, if he hadn't finished it at the office that day. Noan would be busily engaged in the kitchen making dinner. She was almost the world's worst cook, although once in a while she surprised me and even herself! She hadn't worked outside the home since I started high school. I wondered what they would talk about when I was gone. The three of us had lived alone together for the last 20 years, and now I was removed from the picture. Not removed to get a job someplace else. Not removed to get married, but removed to go to war. It was an unpleasant thought. Somehow, I think they realized now that it would never be the same again. When I returned I would be going to college, getting married, and just visiting now and then. For them as well as me, it was the end of an era and the beginning of an uncertain future.

My mother, father and I left for the train station after 2am and got there a few minutes before train time. And there I met Ralph Hogan. He had been in high school with me, although we hadn't been close friends. He had received an identical letter to mine. We had an experience to share, so we were happy to see each other. Someone else was going to be going to Santa Ana besides me!

My father shook my hand as I boarded. My mother held up remarkably well, but I knew it was only because she had absolutely no control over the situation and had to accept what came. But you'd have thought I was going overseas right then and there!

The train left Ukiah for San Francisco at 4am. Next I would take the "Lark" train from San Francisco to Los Angeles

Sunday night.

After arriving in Sausalito, Ralph and I took the ferry across the bay and spent the rest of the day together in San Francisco waiting for the night train to Los Angeles. To pass the time, we went to a movie. I'm not sure about Ralph, but I know I fell asleep. I had gotten virtually no sleep the night before. We had dinner together and then headed out to catch our trains. Unfortunately, Ralph's reservations were on the Owl, a night train leaving from Oakland, and mine were on the Lark, leaving from San Francisco. We said goodbye, never realizing we wouldn't see each other again for more than a year and a half, and then it would be under very different circumstances; upon my arrival at prison camp in Germany. The next time I saw Ralph Hogan we were both POWs!

After arriving at the Union Depot in LA, a rather large group of us (by now) took the old electric train to Santa Ana and were picked up by Army trucks and transported to the Air Base.

When I first got to Santa Ana on December 14, 1942, the base was not yet complete. Eventually, it would hold over 50,000 cadets. Now it was about 2/3 full, and buildings were still being built. The essentials were ready - the barracks, the parade grounds, the mess hall, a 3000-seat theater - all happily close to our squadron's barracks. Some roads still weren't paved, additional barracks were still going up, and whatever was ready for use was brand new. Unfortunately it rained a great deal - it was December, after all. That meant that those unpaved roads turned to mud, although that didn't keep us from marching, marching and more marching. There was a lot of griping about all the marching when we had joined the Air Force to fly!

After I got to Santa Ana, I started getting letters from my mother. She was very regular about sending me all the latest news from Redwood Valley. I never lacked for mail at mail call.

On Christmas Eve, just ten days after our arrival, the powers-that-be decided we needed cheering up.

In those days, America considered itself very "family-oriented." At Christmas, you were supposed to be at home with your family. You didn't just call home and say "Merry Christmas" or just send a card. It would have been sacrilege to miss Christmas with the family. The Army decided we shouldn't be left in our barracks on a cold rainy Christmas Eve to mull over our plight. We fell out in formation about seven that evening. It was raining heavily and the roads were all mud. We marched briskly through the rain and mud about five blocks to a large movie theater that had about 3000 seats. We trudged in, dripping and cold in sodden boots. Fortunately, the heating system worked and we began to dry out. The theater had just recently been finished and not a single movie had been shown there as yet. Tonight there would be no movies either. Instead, the curtains opened and there was a grand piano with a man sitting behind it who was introduced as a well-known Broadway Composer. Then a charming young lady walks out and was introduced as a "well known" vocalist from Hollywood. She wasn't a big star, but she had a pretty good voice. These two people were giving up their Christmas Eve just so they could entertain 3000 lonely soldiers who were all away from home for the first time. She sang her heart out and he played the piano without breaks for almost three hours. I think they covered the entire Hit Parade from the last ten years. And that was it. We weren't expecting Bob Hope... he hadn't yet established his reputation for entertaining the troops. After the performance, we fell out. It was still raining and we marched back through the mud to the barracks.

We cleaned our boots as best we could and returned into the barracks. The floor still got pretty dirty. Right after our breakfast in the mess hall, the next morning, we were told there would be a barracks inspection at 10 o'clock and the floor would have to be scrubbed spotless and our lockers and clothes in perfect order. All that mud on the floor didn't help much. We got to work and the first grousing (a lot more that would ensue over the next four years) started. Yet the barracks were spotless when the inspection came, including the shiniest boots you ever saw. After that, no one wore their boots in the barracks until the roads were paved. You carried them in and washed them in the latrine before putting them back on!

Pre-flight school still wasn't ready, so we marched some more until someone came up with the idea of pre-preflight school to keep us occupied. So we started attending classes which might just as well have been pre-flight, since we repeated the same subjects again later when pre-flight school was opened for our class.

To fill in any unassigned time we might have on our hands the aviation cadets were assigned "mess management." This was more familiarly known in the regular Army as K.P. However, as future flight crew we were all potential officers... and officers just didn't do K.P. Mess Management assignments were made alphabetically and since I was at the bottom of the alphabet, I would always get the last assignment which was generally "garbage detail." We considered the jobs as "waiters" to be the choice positions, but I never got one. On one occasion I got to be "cook's helper," which was just one step ahead of "garbage detail." To add to a new recruit's bewilderment, all the cooks were civilians.

On the day I got to be "cook's helper" I was assigned to a very chubby young civilian cook who put me to work slicing onions. I was carefully slicing them, standing as far back from them as I could, when I noticed that he was slicing more onions over on the next butcher block table. His knife moved so rapidly, it was like a blur, and the onions were neatly sliced. I watched his hand movements and decided I could do that. So I started moving my knife faster and faster. The only thing was that I didn't tell my other hand to move back fast enough, and I soon took a slice out of my finger. I suppose I was not the only one who did something like that, because they had a first aid station right there in the kitchen. I went over and got my finger bandaged. When I came back, he put me to work slicing beets. I figured he did that so that any bleeding wouldn't show on the food.

The second most unwanted assignment was guard duty. No one wanted this, since you were up all night walking the perimeter of the Air Base and wondering what you would do if you met up with a spy trying to sneak under the fence. Or worse, a Japanese invasion on your watch! The second worry of the night was what you would do if you ran into the officer of the guard and he asked you the 7th general order out of the 10 you were required to memorize and you couldn't remember it! That meant more demerits and a worse assignment than guard duty. What was worse than guard duty?

One afternoon, after an hour or so of marching, we had just returned to our barracks when we were called out again and told that enemy planes had been spotted off the coast and we had to evacuate the Air Base. We were instructed to wear our overcoats and be outside in formation in five minutes. Well, as it happened, I had an urge to go to the latrine and that would only get worse on a forced march. So I made a mad dash in there quickly and found I was not the only one with that idea. Then I hurried upstairs to my bunk to pick up my overcoat. While there, I grabbed an apple that I had stashed in my foot locker, just in case we were out in the wilds overnight. I slipped into my coat and was back out in formation exactly in five minutes. You learned to move fast in the Army. Now, if only the Army would move faster for us! Our CO was a young "90-day wonder" 2nd lieutenant. These officers were referred to by that sobriquet because they were trained for just ninety days and then given a commission to work in an administrative capacity in training other airmen. He was, as were most of the "90-day wonders," full of his self importance and not exactly respected by his squadron. He marched us in those damn overcoats out over the landscape to wherever we were going. The sun was hot and we were just about to have a heat stroke when he decided to halt and give us five minutes rest. Just about that time an order came down the line that the bombers were a false alarm. It was safe to go back to the base. So we didn't get our "five." Instead, we about-faced and started back. It finally took a colonel going by in a Jeep to wake up the lieutenant to the fact that his men were dying of heat prostration. He ordered him to "get those men out of those coats." The lieutenant gave him a snappy salute and then continued marching us for another five minutes before calling a halt and having us take off our coats. That was just to show us that "he was still in charge!" All this talk about a Japanese invasion of Southern California did nothing to allay the bad feeling at three o'clock in the morning, walking that lonely perimeter in the dark on guard duty.

Marching is an obsession with the Army. When we first arrived at Santa Ana, we had as CO an old Captain who had been in the Infantry a number of years. He was a very kind man and talked to us at some length about his Army experiences. He was the first officer we had that taught us marching in formation. Every Sunday the entire complement of the air base would form out on the parade grounds. Here I would stand at "parade rest," which was hardly any better than being "at attention," except I were allowed to stand with my feet slightly apart and my hands clasped behind my back. We would be at "parade rest" while each squadron on the base marched before the Commanding General in review. Every now and then, I could see a man keel over and some medics would rush in and cart him away on a stretcher. The ranks would close up and the rest of us wondered when we would pass out from the sun's heat and the lack of circulation while we stood still. Then when it was our turn, we'd be called to attention and marched off to the reviewing stand. Each Group would be reviewed independently and the best squadron in the group would receive the prized "blue ribbon" for that day. Well, our group of beginners won the blue ribbon for our old captain. Later, when we were assigned to our eager young 2nd lieutenant, we never won anything. He took us out and marched our tails off, even on Saturday, which was supposed to be our day off. But all for nothing. And he couldn't understand why.

Eventually I moved on to Primary Training in Visalia. Noan and Virginia came down to visit me when I made the move. This was a relatively short course, and soon after that I was transferred to San Antonio, Texas. I didn't see any of my family again until I graduated from Navigation School and went home on a twelve day leave before I joined my final crew at Davis Monthan field in Tucson, Arizona, and headed overseas.

Everyone in our class got through pre-flight school without washing out and we were eagerly anticipating our Primary Training School assignment. This would be the first time in the air for many of us and by the time we finished Primary, we would be able to solo, take off and land the aircraft, and be ready for larger, faster planes. In Visalia our Primary trainer was going to be a Ryan PT-22. This was not good news.

3
1943
Primary Training

Primary schools were civilian operated but, naturally, direct supervision of the cadets was still under military control. We were lodged in "civilian style" housing with large rooms that accommodated 10 cadets. And, of course, we were assigned to rooms alphabetically, which put ten Wilsons in one room. That made for an interesting time at mail call. In addition to flying instruction we had classroom sessions, one of which was on navigation. I found this a very interesting course and shortly was at the head of the class. We had so many trainees that they were short of flying instructors. The first of our class - alphabetically, of course - were assigned to the regular flight hours, usually first thing in the morning. Those further down the alphabet were given flights later in the day, and those at the end of the alphabet were flown last. By late afternoon, some of the instructors had only one or two students left, and had maybe two hours flying time still available. As a result, I got more flying time per day than the earlier cadets. But, strangely enough, this was not good in my case.

There being a war on and all, the theory was to grind out pilots as fast as the program could do it. So cadets were normally given 8 hours flying time to qualify for solo flying. Because of the extra time I got each day, I found myself rapidly approaching the 8 hour mark and I simply wasn't satisfying the instructor that I was ready to solo. If I had taken it a bit more slowly, I was convinced that I could have accomplished it. But flying for the first time in your life in an open cockpit P-22 was an experience in itself that took some getting used to. The Ryan P-22 was a low winged monoplane and was reputed to be the fastest landing primary training plane in use. At some of the nearby primary schools, they were flying bi-wing Stearman planes which could just about land themselves. But I was flying a Ryan, and try to satisfy the instructor as I might, he decided that I wasn't ready to solo. So, after doing a "test flight" with another instructor, I was, as they said in that era, "washed out." This was a devastating blow to me, since I had never made any plans to be anything else but a pilot. Another of our "ten Wilsons" washed out about the same time and we spent the next few afternoons, while we were waiting for reassignment, drowning our sorrows in chocolate malts at the local ice cream fountain. It's hard to realize, here at the end of the 20th century, that there was a simpler time when there were hardly any drugs, when a surprising number of young men never even drank alcohol, and when a chocolate malt was considered a satisfying drink to calm your senses when your world was falling apart.

About a week after my final flight, we were called in to fill out some of the many Army forms that plague you throughout your service time. This form asked us to list our choices of what other flight positions we would choose to train for. Not being too swift that day, I put down bombardier. Naturally, that was the assignment I would not get! Before I knew what had happened, I received orders to return to Santa Ana to await reassignment to a navigation school. If I had given any thought to what they might choose for me I would have realized that my stellar grades in the navigation class would certainly influence their decision.

We were now up to mid 1943, and I was about to be reassigned to start yet another training program! The war was progressing without us - not too swiftly, but it was moving along. Those of us who were awaiting reassignment began to wonder if we would ever get to see live action. Just to keep us on our toes the

Officer of the Day inspected our barracks the very first morning we arrived. He randomly picked my bed to toss a dime onto. The blanket didn't "ripple". For that I received nine demerits! If you got ten, you automatically drew guard duty. Naturally I kept my bed blanket skin-tight after that experience. Unfortunately during the rest of our stay, he never showed up again!

After a month of waiting, with the daily barracks inspection the only thing we had to worry about, we finally got orders to transfer to San Antonio Army Air Base - not for navigational training, but to wait for yet another reassignment to navigation school. We boarded a troop train loaded with cadets heading for Texas. This was like going to another country. The train moved none too swiftly and often was sidetracked to allow freight trains to go by. It took us an eternity to get to San Antonio. When we got there we were assigned to a tent city. There were about six or eight of us to a tent. I was in the tent only three days when I reported to the hospital with a fever and general bad feeling. I thought it would be something short, perhaps a flu or something, but I was kept there for six weeks with a case of pneumonitis. It wasn't all that bad. After the first three or four days the fever was gone and I felt fine. The hospital food was good, the room was warmer than the tent, I had plenty of company, and we had nothing to do but read and get well—at least for the first three or four weeks. Then they decided I needed to rebuild my strength with exercise. Several recuperating patients started playing volleyball daily, which was great. That, the doctors decided, was not enough. So they took us on some "cross country" hikes that I thought would kill me for sure. That part of Texas looks flat, but it is crisscrossed with hundreds of arroyos, deep little canyons, and, of course, we had to run down one side and up the other over and over again. And Texas heat is another thing to write home about!

In the Army you form friendships quickly, since you may not have much time in any single location. Soldiers were assigned to different training destinations with little advance notice. Well, I had a buddy that had come with me from Santa Ana, and I was hoping we would get assigned to the same navigation school. If I didn't get out of the hospital soon I was sure I'd miss the next class. I felt great and was ready to get out of the hospital as soon as they'd let me. They had this little exercise that they performed daily. An orderly would come in with a wheel chair and insist that you get in it. Then he would wheel you through what seemed like miles of corridors. Then a nurse would draw some blood and he would wheel you back. This went on for weeks. I just accepted it as part of their attempt to cure me of pneumonitis. Later, I found out that they were just using the blood samples for other research and I was merely a healthy donor doing it for the good of my country! On the day I was to go to the doctor for my final examination, I got a serious twinge in my back and I could hardly bend over. I knew that if I told them about it, I'd have to stay another week or two. So, I bluffed my way through the examination. I even bent over, gritting my teeth, not showing any pain. It must have worked, because they discharged me from the hospital!

I got back to my old tent assignment and found my buddy still there. He had spent the last six weeks picking up rocks, clearing the roads and parade grounds. A nice pastime for soldiers breathlessly waiting to get into the hot war! He must have picked up all the rocks, since I never was assigned such a detail. We spent the next few weeks learning to play chess. One of the other cadets in our tent showed us how to play, but his instructions didn't sink in too well. One day we were playing a game and another fellow came over and watched us and said, "Hey! You guys are both in check! You can't just go on moving." We had been moving our pieces around the board, blissfully unaware of the plight of our kings.

Finally our assignments came through. We were being sent to gunnery school in Harlingen, Texas, for six weeks training, since navigation school still wasn't ready.

4
1943
Navigation

I wondered if the German Army went through the same circuitous training regimen that we did; hurry up and wait, hurry up and wait! That was our battle cry. I had a feeling the Germans hurried up but weren't waiting. Gunnery school was an interesting experience; I learned how to operate gun turrets, rifles, shotguns, shoot skeet and trap, and even had air-to-air gunnery practice. I was always glad that I wasn't the pilot towing the target that all these clumsy trainees were shooting at. On the down side of gunnery school was the location. It was situated just south of Harlingen, at Brownsville, Texas, on the Gulf of Mexico. The area was blessed with mosquitoes almost as big as the planes we flew in. The PX was always out of the only mosquito repellent that was on the market in those days, so we had a constant swatting battle with the insects. They had a theater there where they showed current movies. However it had benches in it in place of seats and the dark, humid, terribly warm theater was an excellent place for the mosquitoes to hide and then dive bomb you as soon as the picture started. Needless to say, we went to the movies just one time. In addition to these problems they had the worst mess hall I ever found on any Army base. As far as I could tell every cadet bought "ready-made" sandwiches from a dispensing machine in the PX rather than go to that mess hall.

Our air-to-air gunnery practice was accomplished by flying in a two-engine bomber and firing from the various positions on the plane - the electric top turret, the hand-held waist guns, and the tail turret. I was given belts of 50 caliber ammunition the tips of which had been dipped in a certain colored paint. When I hit the target, the paint would leave a trace of my color and I was awarded a certain number of "hits" on each mission. The next cadet would have a different color. You might think that the sleeve target would soon be riddled with holes, but air-to-air gunnery wasn't very well perfected in those days, and if a cadet got 10% hits he was awarded a sharpshooter's medal. So I tried my best and didn't waste any shots. We had an old Army Sergeant who had somehow gotten into the cadet program, even though he was over the age limit. He was a nice enough fellow, but he couldn't hit the proverbial broad side of a barn if he was standing right in front of it. He was, however, a whiz at Morse Code, which was an additional class they threw at us for some reason we never identified. I could send Morse code fairly well but really struggled at receiving it. One day our sergeant was on one of my flights and I was firing from the top turret, which was my favorite place. I fired my first belt, then loaded my second and fired it. Suddenly it stopped and I thought I had run out, but I must have fired awfully fast to be done so soon. The sergeant followed me in the turret. He seemed to make quite a production of it before he started firing, but finally finished off his rounds. When the plane landed he came over and told me, "You're belt was jammed, but I fixed it and fired the rest of your rounds for you." I smiled dimly and said, "Good for you." Needless to say, I didn't get any 10% hits that day.

    The oppressive heat at Brownsville was probably the worst part of the six weeks experience. There was no air conditioning and after a couple of weeks my pores just gave up and I got what was known as "prickly heat". This was a burning, prickling sensation that I couldn't do anything about except stand in a cold shower and use calamine lotion. Of course, that was another item that the PX was always out of. The perspiration ran down my fingers so badly while I was writing a letter home it smeared the ink.

I could hardly read the words. We spent a lot of time in the showers.

We completed gunnery school, and, amazingly enough, finally got our assignments to navigation school. I was sent to Hondo Air Force Base, about 40 miles west of San Antonio, and my buddy was sent to San Angelo, Texas. That was the last we saw of each other. Now, finally, we came to grips with a course that, if completed successfully, would end with us getting our commissions, our officer's uniforms, and our long awaited assignment overseas. It was November, 1943, just short of a year since I had been called to active duty and I was just about to begin training all over again! The navigation course that seemed so simple in Primary school suddenly became a lot more difficult. We received training in dead reckoning and in celestial navigation. The latter took up the most time and included many night flights where we would navigate by the stars. We used an octant with a bubble level in which I centered the star I was using. Then I proceeded to push a little lever that marked a wax disk on the side of the octant. I did this several times over a given period of time. When I finished, I took an average reading on the side of the disk and marked it down. This was followed by two more readings and then I could triangulate our position on the map. Ideally, the marks were very close together. However, some nights we flew in an old bomber that didn't fly through the sky - it waddled. On those occasions, I frequently found marks on the disk going completely around a full 360 degrees. There was absolutely no stable platform to shoot from.

It was here at Hondo that I met my next short-time buddy. His name was Willie Williams. (Due to alphabetical order, as always, I only got to know people at my end of the alphabet.) Willie and I got along great. We celebrated the weekends by going to dinner at a restaurant on the post and then attending a movie. At that time I could go see the latest hit Hollywood movies at the post theater for 25 cents.

We only went into San Antonio on a weekend pass once. We had to take the train in from Hondo and then make sure to catch the last train back about 11 p.m. On this one weekend in town we visited the Alamo, went for a boat ride down the San Antonio River, and drank gallons of fruit juices at a stand that sold every kind of fruit juice available on the planet. The Texas heat was still overwhelming but between the fruit juice and the rides on the river, we survived the day. We were late getting back to the train station and managed to miss the last train by seconds. We had to get back to Hondo by 4 am or we'd miss bed check. That was pretty serious stuff for such young innocent guys as we were. There was nothing to do but try hitchhiking. Neither of us had any experience at this, but we headed out the highway and hoped for the best. We didn't have too long to wait before a car slowed and stopped. It was an officer returning to Hondo. At first we thought this was great! After a few minutes we realized it might not be. This particular officer had been drinking a lot more than he should have, and his driving was erratic and fast. In short order we were far ahead of the train. We decided that if we got back to the base alive we'd at least be in plenty of time for bed-check. Luckily we accomplished both.

Near the end of our training we were scheduled for a graduation flight that would make us or break us. Fortunately we flew in an AT-7 training plane, not that big old lumbering bomber that waddled across Texas. The test mission flew to Topeka, Kansas, Des Moines, Iowa, and El Paso, Texas. Different cadets were assigned as "lead navigator" on each segment of the trip and each was responsible for giving the pilot instructions. Whoever was not "lead" followed the trip on his maps and projected his own interpretation of the course. When we got to El Paso, a dust storm came up, blotting out the sky up to 30,000 feet. We had never seen anything like it and it delayed our take off several days. When we finally got away from El Paso we were so late that we were scheduled to land at Hondo just a few hours before the graduating ceremonies. None of us on the plane even knew if we had passed or not. Still in the dark, we reported to our squadron office and were given instructions for picking up our uniforms for graduation. We fell into formation at the given time and marched to the parade ground where the ceremony was taking place. We never found out if we passed that final flight, but we guessed we must have, because the next thing we knew, we were all wearing 2nd Lieutenant's bars on our uniforms and were given twelve days leave to go home before reporting to Davis-Monthan Field in Tucson, Arizona, to be assigned to our overseas crew. At long last!

    I was prepared when I graduated from Navigation School to fly back to San Francisco for a leave to visit home. During the last six weeks of our training we were told to make our airline reservations to go home on our 12 day leave after graduation. I dutifully made my reservations on Braniff Air Lines from San Antonio to Dallas, and on American Air Lines from Dallas to San Francisco. If you got reservations you were considered to be quite fortunate, since travel by air was hard to get. There was always someone waiting in case you canceled or couldn't make a trip for one reason or another. Well, I got to San Antonio early that fateful morning, checked in with Braniff and waited. This was the story of my military experience - wait, wait, wait. It seems as though Braniff had engine trouble with the plane that was taking us to Dallas.

There were no other flights scheduled, and no other planes available. We were supposed to take off for Dallas at 7 am. The plane finally left at 10 am and my hopes of meeting my American Flight in Dallas were shattered. When we got there my flight for California had long since left and there just were no other flights going my way that day. All of the flights for the next several days were booked solid. I didn't want to sit around hoping someone would cancel, so I did the only thing possible when you are stuck deep in the heart of Texas. I took the Atchison, Topeka, & The Santa Fe! I got a berth so that I could at least get some decent rest. This train trip took up five days of my twelve day leave and I was understandably upset! We left shortly after I got my ticket and chugged our way across the country, each mile passing maddeningly slowly as the train pulled off on sidings and waited for freights going the other way. Of course, this was a passenger train and freight trains had the right of way (there was a war on, you know!) Each time two trains were approaching each other on the same track we pulled over on a siding and waited endlessly for the freight to chug past. Those delays seemed a lot longer than they were. I watched my twelve days leave dwindling away. It was not a fun trip. I did eventually get home and spent just short of a week with my family before heading back to Arizona and my new crew assignment.

During this train trip, staring out the window and watching the Texas and New Mexico scenery roll slowly past, a my mind dwelled upon a single question at some length. What bomber would I be assigned to - a B-17 or a B-24? Now, many decades later, that seems like a very silly thing to be dwelling upon. However it was - at the time - the hot topic among graduates in our class. Everyone seemed to favor the B-17. It was considered the "glamour" ship of the early war years. B-24s had only recently gone into production on a large scale and none of us knew much about them. As it turned out, we would be trained at Davis-Monthan in B-24s.

My reporting date to Tucson was still a week away when my train from Los Angeles to San Francisco arrived at its destination. My folks came down from Ukiah to pick me up and we had a great family reunion when we got home. I had been gone just 18 months, and with all the celebrating, one would think I had already won the war single handed.

When my day to leave arrived - much too quickly - I again boarded the train to San Francisco, and then got the earliest train possible to Los Angeles. There I changed trains again for Tucson. For once in my entire military career, the timing for these transfers worked out rather well. When I reported in at Davis-Monthan, I signed in and the number assigned to me was my new crew number. If I had been ahead of the Lieutenant in front of me I would have been assigned to his crew, which I later learned were not the best in the squadron. Fate smiled upon me that day and I was assigned to a great crew headed up by our first pilot, Myron Hood Donald, who quickly became known as "Don". Our co-pilot was Frank Smith and our bombardier was Teddy Emens. Frank was the only other Californian on the crew. It took a while to get to know the enlisted men, since we were only together when we flew a training mission.

We flew a *lot* of training missions. We "bombed" the Arizona dessert with bags of flour that were aimed at "bull's eye" targets outlined on the ground. We could get a quick answer that way regarding how close we were to the target. We also attended ground school classes to familiarize us with the B-24. We had celestial navigation exercises in ground training facilities where the stars moved across a dome where I tracked them for a four hour mission. Teddy and I took bombing exercises on a trainer located in a huge hangar. The navigator (that would be me) was considered "backup" in case anything happened to the bombardier and had to know the basics of bombing. The trainer consisted of four legs about 12 feet tall with a platform on top and wheels on the bottom. The wheels were motor driven and moved the rig inch by inch across the hangar floor. We sat on top of the platform and operated the Norden bombsight by viewing the "landscape" that was painted on the floor below. The speed of the movement was linked to the bombsight and I dropped my "bombs" at the given release point as indicated by the speed I was traveling. Unfortunately, the hangar floor had been poured in large sections, and every place there was a joint in the concrete the whole rig jerked and threw off the speed, so you never knew exactly when you reached the release point. It was not the greatest tool for training!

We enjoyed the warm spring evenings in Tucson with the scent of orange blossoms filling the valley. The four of us - Don, Frank, Teddy and I - went into town in the evenings, had dinner and spent some time in a local pub. We discussed the war, how it was progressing and whether or not we'd ever actually get into combat. The enlisted men formed their own group when it came to social activities, but when it came time to fly a mission we were one united group, determined to be the best crew in the squadron. We still had no idea where we would be sent to serve. The Army was very secretive about these things and B-24's were used in both the Pacific and European theaters. So we practiced and waited. Finally the day came; we were given orders to go to Lincoln, Nebraska, where we were to pick up a brand new ship right off the assembly line. This should have given us a clue, since B-24's were also built on the west coast. But we still weren't sure

5
1944
Across The Sea

We left Davis-Monthan by train once again. The tracks went right through the air base, so we boarded right there with a host of "permanent party" military to see us off. I remember one particular Lt. Colonel, who none of us particularly cared for, saying, "Drop one for me, boys!" I think the general consensus of opinion was to drop one on *him!* It was a typical warm Sunday morning when the train pulled out. It seemed to move faster than any of the other train trips I had made. We decided Eisenhower was waiting for us and we'd better get moving. That was the direction we were going and that's the way it turned out.

We had visions of arriving at Lincoln, filling out the usual forms, and picking up our plane and flying away. Hadn't we learned anything by now? We arrived, filled out the usual forms, and we were actually assigned to a new aircraft- but then we had to "get to know the new plane." This was accomplished through - yes - another series of training missions, one of which was known as "swinging the compass." In this little exercise, the pilot followed a prescribed course outlined on the ground. If that course was due north, then you read your compass, and if it was off one way or another, you noted the deviation. Then he would head off 10 degrees to the right and you'd check the compass again, and so on, until you had gone around a full 360 degrees. Certain magnetic fields within the aircraft caused these deviations, so it had to be done while the plane was actually in flight.

Our plane was a very bright and shiny brand new aluminum-covered B-24. The Army had stopped painting them an olive drab some months back. I don't think the olive drab color ever helped to "hide" them from attacking fighters anyway. Besides, from what we had heard, there were fewer and fewer German Fighters in the air these days. Our predecessors had taken out most of the fighters, bases, and manufacturing plants, in the last year or so.

After about two weeks of flying our new plane we received orders to proceed to Grenier Field, New Hampshire. This was the order that finally made our destination clear. We were going to Europe. Planes were taking off constantly, heading out to Grenier, Presque Isle, Maine, and other northeastern bases. So this was finally it. It was an exciting moment for our crew, who had now been augmented by a new radio man. Our old radio man had gone off base, imbibed a bit too heavily, and never got back in time. A new and presumably more responsible man was assigned to us. It was a definite improvement. He was a handsome young eager airman named Jack Stidham. He was very personable and did his job much more thoroughly than our old crewman. This made our crew a truly complete unit and we got along like a family.

We landed in the green hills of New Hampshire, and I was overwhelmed by the beauty of New England. We never got off the base, since our departure could occur on a moment's notice, but the immediate area surrounding the field was something I would always remember. Perhaps it was just a little bit of home I wanted to take with me.

We were only there a couple of days when we received our next orders to proceed to Goose Bay, Labrador, Canada. We were slowly creeping up the eastern edge of North America.

On the morning of our departure my pilot and I were ordered to the briefing room while the rest of the crew took our gear and stowed everything away on our aircraft. We received our flight instructions and were warned that we had better not go down in the great Canadian North Woods, since people could be lost permanently in that vast area.

When we got on the plane and taxied out for takeoff I discovered that our co-pilot, Frank Smith, had somehow managed to lose my travel case, which held all those important items of your life, like a razor, toothbrush, comb, etc. The truck taking the crews out to the flight line carried two or three crews and somehow my case had gotten mixed up with their luggage and was now on the way to God knows where. As New England fell away and we left U.S. soil for the last time all I could think about was how I was going to brush my teeth.

A B-24 generally had a crew of 10. There was the pilot, co-pilot, navigator, bombardier, nose gunner, two waist gunners, tail gunner, radio man and engineer. However, unless you were a lead ship in a squadron, or deputy lead, the bombardier sat in the nose turret where he could see the bombs being salvoed by the lead ship and then salvo the bombs in his ship remotely. Therefore, you didn't need another nose gunner - he was it. So we had only 9 on board. Teddy decided to stay up on the flight deck. We had a long flight to make and all my computations were in order, so I had nothing to do but sit up in the nose turret and enjoy the flight.

The nose turret on a B-24 was all glass with a 300 degree unobstructed view - and what a magnificent view it was! We crossed the St. Lawrence River and immediately were over dense forest. It could have been a South American jungle; it was so thick and green. We flew for hours over this magnificent country. The nose turret, of course, was situated well in front of the wings and the engines, so it was as though I was out there floating across the landscape, with just the gentle hum of the engines behind me. Fighter planes were still two thousand miles away. There was no flak to worry about. I just enjoyed the flight.

When we got to Goose Bay it was now early June, but the landscape still was fairly well covered with snow. When we got off the plane we noticed the drop in temperature immediately. We were in the northern latitudes. The crew was assigned to a well built two story barracks which was equipped with steam heat. There was a great mess hall with some of the best food I had found in the Army. The first place I looked for was a PX. I had to find some things to replace my losses at Grenier. Naturally, there was a war on, so the items I found were not exactly what I lost. The razor was made out of plastic and I was sure I wasn't going to get a close shave out of it.

We were getting so close to combat that each delay seemed an eternity. The layover at Goose Bay lasted several days as we waited for the weather to clear over Iceland, which was our next stop. Finally we got the okay and went into the briefing room where they gave us the wind and the weather reports. The flight plan, of course, took us over the Atlantic Ocean, so I had nothing to navigate by. I took the wind report, planned the flight to a certain degree of longitude, made one correction and zeroed in on Reykjavik.

That was the theory, anyway. It turned out to be a very dull flight. We had a solid undercast of low clouds all the way across to Iceland. We never saw a wave, a boat, or any sign of life until we got about ten miles from the island. Then, suddenly, the clouds opened up like curtains in a theater when the performance is about to begin and there was the ocean. Straight ahead, almost perfectly lined up, was the runway at Reykjavik. I would have been proud of my navigational skills, except I owed our accurate flight to the weatherman.

Now it was the 3rd of June and we were stuck in Iceland. The word was that the weather was really "socked in" in Ireland, where we were landing next, and we'd have to wait for it to clear. In Iceland in June the sun never sets. Well, that is not entirely true. It dips down below the horizon for maybe 10 minutes and then brightly returns to its duties. As a result it is never dark and due to the round-the-clock poker games the crews played everyone lost track of time. That is - everyone except one little dog who was one of the crews' mascots. He slept during the PM and was wide eyed during the day shift. Everyone checked with him to see what time

---

LETTER HOME - *June 9, 1944*

Dear Mom 'n Pop,

By the time you get this it should be "Happy Birthday to Noan!" Anyway, I hope you get this by then. We are still moving around and all we are free to say at the moment is that we are somewhere in Iceland - not permanent, thank heavens! It's never dark here and I'm constantly in a daze as to whether it is morning, noon, or night! The sun does go down for about two hours, but it's no darker for those two hours than it is at home around 7pm on a summer eve. You sure can't get your directions here either, with the sun rising, going around in a circle, and setting right back where it came from.

Had a catastrophe at one of the fields leaving the U.S. - I lost my musette bag, which held of the the wonderful little things that make life possible - - my complete shaving kit - the one you gave me - my manicure scissors, bottle of kreme, soap, face clothes, handkerchiefs, gum, writing kit, and worst my list of mailing addresses! I managed to replace the most necessary items like razor and toothbrush, but it sure was a blow to morale!

I hope you had a happy birthday, Noan! And have an extry good Papa's Day, Pop!

Bye now,
Brad

it was.

Three days later, on June 6th, we got the earth-shattering news; the allied invasion of Europe had been launched (the event subsequently referred to as "D-Day," although not at the time.) The allies had stormed Normandy and were moving inland. The crew was, to a man, very upset! We weren't there for the biggest moment in history! Instead we were stuck in Iceland! The general consensus was that the war would now be over before we got into it. (In hindsight this was admirable optimism!) Just in case there was any resistance, the Army decided to send us over anyway - to sort of clean things up. So on June 9th we headed for Ireland.

I could clearly see why it was called the Emerald Isle. We had no trouble finding it. It glistened like an emerald in the blue sea. It was a beautiful sight. As soon as we got to our destination - which was Shannon - I joined the rest of the crew on the flight deck and showed the pilot my map and pointed to what seemed to be hundreds of airports all crammed into a small area. Don had to pick out the right one, with a little help from the ground.

We were whisked with our baggage to a Quonset hut and I got my introduction to a mummy style sleeping bag. We never saw our beautiful new shiny plane again. Apparently we had just ferried it over and it would be sent on to the modification hanger and then on to somewhere it was needed, while we would be scheduled for - you guessed it - more training.

I'm sure you're asking why a brand new B-24 was sent to a modification hangar before being sent into action. Why would the military modify a brand new plane right off the assembly line?! Well, evidently no one told the builders back home that they weren't using "Sperry Ball Turrets" anymore in the European Theater. And, since the enemy fighters had been trimmed back considerably, they decided to remove the "coffin seats" used by the

77

pilot and co-pilot. These seats got their name from the design. They were built of heavy gauge steel in the shape of a coffin that surrounded the back, head and shoulders of the pilots and protected them from errant rounds that might have otherwise hit them. These steel protectors were cut out with an acetylene torch. After these modifications, the planes were then released to the waiting squadrons in England.

We were only in Shannon for one night, although that was enough. We slept on cots in the Quonset huts in the aforementioned sleeping bags. In case you're not familiar with "mummy" sleeping bags; these bags are shaped wide at the shoulder and then tapering down to a narrow point at the feet. Once I was inside there was no way I could bend or move my legs. This was not good for someone who moves his legs continually

---

LETTER HOME - *June 11, 1944*

Dear Mom 'n Pop,

I don't know the number of missions my currently crew will fly together, but I hope the ten of us will remain a team until our flying job is done. Our co-pilot is really dependable, which is hard to say about most co-pilots. Most co-pilots are mad at the world because they aren't first pilots. F.C., the boy from Oakand, has a cold - he doesn't want to go on sick call here and get us all stuck in Iceland indefinitely. And if they did put him in the hospital they might give us another co-pilot, and that's no good. So F.C. spends 20 hours a day in bed and we await the moments when they hand us a flight plan and we take our plane to... well, someplace or other, I'm sure I'm not allowed to say!

Bye now, folks!
Brad

during a good night's sleep. I barely got a moment's rest.

At dawn we were trucked to a port on the Irish Sea where we boarded a boat for England. We landed quite far north, near Scotland, and then boarded a train for Norwich. The English countryside was so calm and beautiful. It was hard to think about the fact that this very country was being subjected to continuous bombing. But we'd see evidence of that soon enough.

When we arrived at a base, we were stashed away in a barracks for only a couple of days before our orders same through. Finally, we thought, we would be assigned to a bombing group and see some action. This was a few weeks after D-day and the war was still on. Well, we'd bring it to a hasty conclusion. But the orders were not assigning us to a fighting squadron; they were sending us *back* to Ireland for more training! We'd just come from there, and now were on the way back. It is, at times, hard to figure out the ways of the Army.

That morning we were brought down to the flight line and loaded into an old B-24 that had seen so much service that it had been retired to serve as a taxi. The rules required the flight crew to be on the flight deck at takeoff and landing, firmly strapped in by their seat belts on a bench. No one was to ride in the nose of the ship. Overseas, we quickly learned rules were bent a bit as needs dictated. In this case, they had to load a dozen crews on board to fly back to Ireland. Crewmen were stashed on the flight deck, in the bomb bay, in the waist of the ship - anyplace they could squeeze in. I was jammed into the nose of the ship right up against the glassed-in nose that had preceded the models with gun turrets. I looked down and there was the runway staring at me from only a couple of feet away. When we took off, the whole ship vibrated like every rivet and bolt was loose (they probably were). The runway sped by under my gaze at a frightening speed. That was the least of my worries on this short trip.

Shortly thereafter we arrived over the air strip in Ireland and the ship came down, tires screeching as they hit the runway, and we rolled once again at frightening speed over the concrete. Unfortunately we weren't slowing down. I could see the end of the runway up ahead and I wondered if the pilot did. We felt the brakes being applied, but the plane continued to roll hell-bent for disaster in a mossy Irish bog. We heard the pilot reverse the props and the plane shuddered like it was about to burst apart. But the speed continued and I said to myself, "One hell of a way to end the war before I even get into it!" There it was, looming up just ahead of us - the end of the runway. A barbed wire fence seemed the only thing that could save us now, and I somehow didn't think it would hold. Then, at precisely the last minute, the pilot, who I assumed had done this many times before, whipped that plane in a left turn that should have ripped it apart. Suddenly we were taxiing down a ramp at a fair to normal speed. We were once again in Ireland.

This time, at least, we did not encounter any "mummy" bags. We were assigned to our quonset hut in the beautiful Irish countryside. We quickly learned that you never left your hut without your umbrella. It rained daily, several times a day, with bright beautiful sunshine glistening off the emerald colored moss all around the walks, in between showers. If you stepped on the moss, any time, day or night, it squished softly. Ireland was one wet place.

What did we miss in our training? What could we possible learn that hadn't been drummed into our heads by now? Well, there was formation flying. That was never demonstrated back in the states, so we had to learn how to "form on the lead ship" and how to hold our formation, when to close up, when to spread out and how not to run into the next guy while you were doing it. And that did happen occasionally. Once, after we were at our permanent base, I was walking to the officers' club about 10 a.m. and some B-17's were going up into formation. I couldn't figure out what they were doing, forming this late in the day. Most of our missions were around 6am - just about dawn. Anyway, these 17's were forming, and suddenly one took too wide a turn and ran into his wing man. Both planes began spiraling down out of control. Immediately, we saw parachutes begin to blossom as the crew bailed out. We counted all the chutes we could see, but they didn't add up to the crews' total.

What a miserable feeling that accident gave us. It was a

LETTER HOME - *June 16, 1944*

Dear Mom 'n Pop,

I suppose you know where I am by now. They told us that the notice would appear in our home town papers before the letters arrived. However, lest the Redwood Journal missed the boat and didn't print the not-so-startling news, I am in that place where all good little airmen go to test their wings and prove they are made of the indestructible stuff little airmen's wings are made of! Yes, I am "somewhere in England." The army insists I say "somewhere in England," although that seems superfluous. I'd rather just say "England," as you know doggone well I am somewhere as opposed to nowhere.

They say we may make a general reference to the weather, so I'll sum it up in one word - stinko! It's raining everyplace in England, so I don't suppose it narrows my location down if I say it is raining here. The countryside is as green as a two-day recruit. More news after I settle in!

Bye now,
Brad

perfectly cloudless morning, rare over Great Britain, and there was no reason for something like that to happen. *Take care* and *fly by the rules of formation flying* became my motto.

6
1944
The 445th

For the next two weeks we flew in formation every day, up and down Ireland, over the Irish Sea, over the Atlantic, but keeping well to the west of the combat zone. At the end of our training period, we were flown back once again to England, to a base near Norwich, where most of them were. The base was located next to the tiny village of Tibenham. This was to be our home for our tour in the European Theater - the 445th Bomb Group. We were assigned to the 702nd Squadron, which had been under the command of one Jimmy Stewart, who had by this time gone on to greater things, unfortunately for us. It would have been great to go home after the war and tell everyone Jimmy Stewart was our CO.

By now one would think that our training was over. It was not. One training mission flying over England was required

from Brad Wilson's **STALAG LUFT 1 P.O.W. JOURNAL, 1945**

Myron Donald, Frank Smith, Teddy Emens, Brad Wilson, Anthony Kielar, Jack Stidham, James McEntee, Lawrence Modlin, Walt Walston, Cox (don't recall his first name) - that was the way the loading list read on the plane that flew us overseas and the same crew flew on the Dixie Flyer some months later. But soon Cox was dropped and after a number of missions Teddy and I temporarily joined Webster and Sherman. We were to go back to our original crew a little later and never quite made it.

before we were scheduled to go into combat. We were assigned to the ever present Quonset huts, our enlisted men in one and the officers in another. There were officers from several crews in our hut and we were treated like the "green guys" we were and had to listen to tales of missions that we soon enough would be experiencing first hand. It was only about a five minute walk to the mess hall and the officers' club from our hut, but it was tricky at 4 o'clock in the morning, in complete darkness with no lights to guide you and occasional airmen zipping by on a bicycle going god-knows-where. Somehow our eyes became accustomed to it and we could pick up enough shapes to navigate through the obstacles without a calamity.

It would certainly be difficult to ever forget that first mission. I generally knew the night before if my crew was scheduled for a mission the next day. This usually required me to hit the sack a bit earlier than normal, since the CQ would come storming through our hut about 2:30 am waking all the crews who that were scheduled for that day. He generally wasn't too well liked. It was quite a shock that first morning, even though I knew it would happen. And in spite of all the training and in spite of our long delayed enthusiasm to get into the fray, now that it was here there was a slight apprehension, a tightness in my belly and in my chest. This was really it. Here we go....

We hustled out to the latrine, me with my new shaving equipment, and got shaved, combed and dressed. Then we tackled the walk to the mess hall which seemed a lot farther than it had in the daylight. Breakfast consisted, as usual, of reconstituted dried eggs, bacon, toast, coffee, and sometimes sweet rolls that weren't very heavy on the sweet. I could have had mush instead of eggs (I say mush rather than oatmeal, because the grain used was difficult to identify.) As bad as the eggs were, they were preferable to the mush. We soon finished breakfast and the officers went to the briefing room and the enlisted men went to the plane. This meant that the enlisted men were still "in the dark" as to what our mission would be until we joined them and were airborne. It probably didn't make much difference to the gunners. Whatever the target, their target was any enemy planes we might encounter.

The briefing usually took about an hour. We were told what our target was for the day and got a lecture on what to expect over our target; flak, enemy fighters, heavy clouds, etc. Then this was followed by a lengthy briefing by the weatherman, which was seldom accurate in those days. We wanted to hear the word CAVU, which meant "ceiling and visibility unlimited." That was at least what the navigator wanted to hear. Among the various things we had learned about on our many training missions since coming to England was a device called the "G-BOX". It was a navigational tool that we could use over the English Channel and even over the continent for a short ways if the signals weren't jammed - sort of a local, 1940s version of GPS. Generally, however, the Germans did a pretty neat job of jamming those signals, so it wasn't much help until you got about halfway across the channel on the way home. Over the European continent you had only two choices—accept the wind drift information given to you by the weather man or use pilotage or dead reckoning—meaning, read your map and follow your progress by looking at the landscape below. The maps were very accurate and easy to follow, but if you had a cloud layer beneath you, you were just out of luck.

Our first mission turned out to be the longest mission of our entire tour of duty. We were being sent to bomb an air base in Ulm, Germany, which was located in the southeastern corner of the country. The flight lasted a full nine hours. When we reported to our plane, each of us went to his own work station to get hooked up and strapped in. My first big surprise was that I didn't have a seat to sit on. The navigator's desk was situated in the nose of the ship directly behind the nose turret. He had a "sling seat" that was hooked up to both sides of the airplane. Mine was missing. I jumped out of the plane and went over to the ground crew chief and told him. He said he'd find me "something". I didn't like the sound of that, but I went back to my station and started getting organized. It was still completely dark outside. We didn't take off until there was enough light to see how to form on your lead ship. The process of "getting organized" entailed putting on your electric boots, plugging them into your suit, plugging your suit into the plane's electrical system, hooking up your oxygen mask to the proper line, hooking up your intercom line, strapping on your throat mike. When you were all connected up, you didn't move around much. Your chest-pack parachute was always at the ready, close to your feet. Your flack helmet was supposed to be on your head, but often was on top of your chute until you got into enemy territory. I was about as ready as I could get until I could sit down. About that time, the chief came up through the nose-wheel door carrying an orange crate! This, he told me, was the only thing he could find at the moment. The sling seat that had been in the plane had somehow disappeared. So, on the longest flight over Germany that I ever made, I would be doing my best sitting on an orange crate. It was better than standing.

It was an excellent flight for a first mission. We saw not a single German fighter and we encountered not a single burst of flak. It was the proverbial "milk run." I had ample time to experiment with my G-Box and plot our course to Ulm and back. It would have been, as I said, a long and somewhat boring flight, if it hadn't been over enemy territory. There was always that threat hanging over us that something might develop at any time. We landed back at the 445th in late afternoon, disentangled ourselves from our various connections and piled out of the plane to be met by a truck that would take us back from the flight line to the debriefing room. You were briefed in the morning before you left and debriefed in the afternoon when you returned. We had little to report except that we had clearly seen what had appeared to be a deserted air base at Ulm. Not a plane in sight. We dropped our bombs and dug plenty of post holes all over the runways and then turned westward and headed home. "Each mission should be that easy!" the other crews told us.

Our second flight was scheduled the next day. The routine of the day before was repeated and we set off for our planes after the briefing. It again was a relatively easy flight. However, I looked out the window as we neared the target and saw little puffs of smoke about 3 thousand feet below us. These were the explosions of flak being sent our way, but their gunners were a bit off on our altitude. The B-24's flew almost all their missions at 27,000 feet. B-17's flew at 24,000 feet. Perhaps the German gunners thought they were dealing with a division of B-17's. I don't know what the reason was, but over the next 16 missions, they often exploded their flak below us. But on my 17th mission, they unfortunately corrected their error.

By the time we had flown four or five missions, we earned a three day pass in London. The whole crew went as a group, enlisted men and officers. The Army didn't care what you did on leave; you just couldn't socialize on base. We took the train from Norwich down to London and as we neared the city, we began to see the devastation that five years of bombing had done to the largest city on Earth. There were tall buildings that were just skeletons, standing without windows, roofs, or doors. One wondered why the walls were still up. But as we got nearer the center of town, things began looking almost normal, with only an occasional area bomb-blasted. We stayed at a hotel in the heart of Piccadilly. There were theaters, restaurants, lots of hotels and stores and

---

LETTER HOME - *July 3, 1944*

Dear Mom 'n Pop,

So, you said the Redwood Journal said what we were doing over here. What did they say? That's army logic for you - we can't say what' happening to us, but they can have it printed in the newspaper!

Noan, the rows along the ten acres of grapes were always that short. None of them have been removed! Stop fretting.

The following is written by my pilot:

[The next page of the letter is written in a different hand, presumably that of Captain Myron Hood Donald - Ed.]

Dear Mrs. Wilson,

I just want to add a line to Bradford's letter to let you know that he is just as "ornery" as ever - even more so! Honestly, he even ends up with most of my rations - will you ask him to please not swindle me out of most of my sweets? All kidding aside, Mrs. Wilson, he - as well as the rest of us - is getting along swell and we are having lots of good times together.

Sincerely,
Myron Donald

[The letter returns to Brad's handwriting.]

Postscript: The above mentioned rations refer to the three bars of candy, three packages of cookies, one can of peanuts and one package of gum we receive each week. And it's the other way around! I'm just too generous for my own good, I suppose!

Bye now,
Brad

people going about their business like there was no war. This was now the era of the buzz bomb. Hitler had given up trying to destroy British morale by dive bombing. Instead he used this new

---

LETTER HOME - *July 4, 1944*

Dear Folks,

Just a year ago today I was resting peacefully in the hospital at San Antonio. It seems like only yesterday - the hot Texas summer, the cool wards - nothing to do but lay in bed and read or write letters. I am missing that Texas heat! Here it is always raining! And I can't dash down to the hospital PX to get a delicious, creamy chocolate malt.

Two years ago today we put in a block of cement out by the kitchen and wrote the date in it. I wish I could take just a few hours break with you to enjoy the summer and go swimming.

I celebrated the Fourth by receiving SEVEN letters from home! That made it a holiday all by itself. Myron got not one, not two, not seven, but TWENTY letters.... I say, TWENTY letters, today.

The old alarm clock Bebe Snow gave me used to always lose time, remember? Ever since I brought it over here it keeps perfect time! It must have been a British clock all along and we just didn't know it!

One more thing you should know because lots of things happen in love and war, and this is war; In the event that we would ever have to bail out over the continent we would probably be listed as missing. In that event my bonds would not continue, but my allotment to the bank would. Just so you know. Meanwhile, I'd probably be high-tailing it for a neutral country! It probably won't happen, kids, but I thought you ought to know!

Bye now,
Brad

scare tactic. This "blind" bomb would fly across the channel from the coast of France, aimed generally in the direction of central London, with limited fuel. When the fuel was consumed, the engine would quit and the bomb would plummet into whatever

---

LETTER HOME - *July 31, 1944*

Dear Mom 'n Pop,

I recently spent a forty-eight hour pass in London. I shall not be going there again on future passes. It would make me a nervous wreck! Not that the buzz bombs are so thick or a great menace to any individual, but they are disquieting to the nerves.

The people of London have an admirable amount of nerve to put up with them. The sirens sound an alert and no one pays any attention to it. Then in about five or ten minutes the drone of the bomb is audible as it comes overhead. It keeps getting louder and then the sound diminishes slowly as it passes. Suddenly the sound stops and the silence that follows is the most terrifying experience endured so far in this war. After about twenty or thirty seconds that seem like an eternity there is the dull thud of an explosion as the bomb lands in another part of the city.

On the second night Theo and I had just gone to bed when we heard that familiar drone. We both jumped up and ran to the window to look out. There in the distance we saw flames from a bomb streaking across the sky coming our way. I said, "Praise the Lord and keep the engine running!" The noise grew louder and the flame streaked closer and darned if that freakish nightmare didn't pass right over our hotel with the engine purring smoothly and it had just gone a few blocks farther when it cut out. We strained our ears as it glided through the darkness and the explosion occurred. After that I thought we would be safe for the night because it seems they never send two over the same area.

Bye now,
Brad

lies beneath. The advice was that if you could hear it going overhead you were safe. But if he engine cut out while it was still approaching, you had better head for a bomb shelter. There was always an air raid alarm to let you know when one or more were coming over.

We checked into our hotel and then we all piled into a taxi and told the driver we wanted to see London. He was veryhappy to oblige and took us to every sight we had ever read about. After we had toured most of the city, he deposited us in front of Madame Tussaud's Wax Museum. We, of course, had all heard of Madame Tussaud's and were looking forward to seeing the real exhibit. Once inside, after visiting a group of historical figures, we came across just about every American motion picture star that we had ever seen. Also greeting us in his typical stance was Joe Louis, then heavyweight boxing champion of the world, having even beat the tar out of the German Max Schmelling a few years back. This was much to Hitler's displeasure, since he was der fuehrer of das master race, and to have a black man beat a German was unthinkable to the racist Reich. This was twice he had been bested by a black man—the first time was when Jesse Owens won a race that included German participants at the 1936 Olympics and which had been held in Berlin, no less.

From the wax museum we returned to the hotel before setting out for a restaurant and dinner. We were rather curious to find out what these restaurants could possibly serve with the strict wartime rationing that was in effect. After all, not much food could be grown on this island-nation, especially with most of the populace engaged in wartime activities. A great deal of the food they had was shipped in from America and had to get by Hitler's u-boats. Well, we soon to found out. We picked out an attractive large restaurant near the hotel and went in. It certainly wasn't crowded, but somehow they managed to survive. We looked at the menu they provided and were surprised to see that one of the choices was roast beef. I wondered how they managed that, since meat was closely rationed even back in the US. So I ordered it and waited to see what arrived. Well, no one ever said the English were known for their good cooking and I suspect they were right. But when the beef arrived, it looked like it had been sliced with a sharp razor. It couldn't have been more than $1/32^{nd}$ of an inch thick. You could see through it to read the menu, if you tried. The gravy looked good, but had about as much flavor as you'd expect. Mashed potatoes and a vegetable of some sort completed the meal, together with sliced bread. As far as the cuisine was concerned, we were going to be glad to get back to the base. We asked about desserts after the meal and the waitress said, "You yanks must have your sweets!" and gave us a big smile as she handed us the menu. They had chocolate pudding listed—well, why not? We ordered the chocolate pudding. If anything was more strictly rationed than meat, it was sugar. I don't think the British saw a teaspoon of sugar during the whole war. She brought the "sweets" which were small cups of something that certainly looked like chocolate pudding. We tasted it and decided the only sweetening that had been put into this pudding was perhaps the little finger of the prettiest girl in the kitchen. We paid the bill and left a friendly tip. She couldn't help the food that was served.

After dinner we strolled around Piccadilly. So did all the English "ladies of the evening" who were out trolling for customers. You could spot them in an instant. They were the only women in Great Britain wearing nylon stockings. At that time of year we were on "double British summer time", which meant it didn't get dark until about 11:30 p.m., so it was easy to see everyone that passed. They all wore expensive clothes and were well made up. There was nothing shy about them. They'd stare right at you as you went by until you made eye contact and then give you a most warm affectionate smile. I'm sure they had as much business as they could handle.

The next morning we went to Harrods. At that time, it was the biggest department store just about anywhere. Don decided to get a new jacket for his dress uniform. They referred us to a tailor just down the street, and Don went in and got measured and then

---

LETTER HOME - *July 19, 1944*

Dear Mom 'n Pop,

I was walking along a path here on the field this evening and as I passed under an old apple tree (of which there are three or four around just loaded with little green apples) I took a deep breath of the country air and closed my eyes and sure enough I thought I was walking through Bill Finne's old grain field. The grass is getting ripe and is slowly beginning to turn, despite all of the rain. It gives such a wonderful scent to the air. There are some wild blackberries here, growing along the path, much like the ones near our place on the path to the river. The blackberries are blooming and on one of the blossoms a little bee was sitting, working away something fierce. He was quite an ordinary little bee, although I imagine the experts would say he was, specifically, an "English bee." So many miles from California and yet here was a little bee that might have come from our own hive! I suppose it was the sunshine today that made this day seem so much nicer.

It gets dark around 11:15pm, but that's because they have two extra hours of daylight saving time over here. The long days are nice and I hate to think of them getting shorter soon.

Bye now,
Brad

spent an hour or two listening to the "tales of the tailor," a very interesting chap who gave us more information on London than any one person has a right to know! I decided to go to a movie down the street from the hotel. They had a seperate theater that showed just newsreels on the war and assorted other short subjects. While I was in the theater watching the show I heard the air raid siren blow outside. No one in the theater showed any interest in leaving, so I decided this must be as good a place as any to wait out the air raid. The show ended and I walked out and went back to the hotel, fully educated on how the war was going! The all-clear siren was blowing. No buzz bomb for Piccadilly that day. I went up to our room and saw a very strange sight. Our bed had six pairs of legs protruding from underneath. I bent down and saw a gaggle of airmen sheepishly trying to extricate themselves from under the bed as unobtrusively as possible. It seems that when the air raid went off they weren't quite sure what to do, so getting under the bed seemed like a good thing to do at the time. Though how that bed was going to protect them if a buzz bomb hit no one seemed to know.

At the end of our leave we took a taxi back to the train station and headed for Norwich. London was enjoyable, but we were actually looking forward to eating at the mess hall.

Over the next two months from the time of our first mission, we flew 16 missions, with number 17 coming up shortly. Clearly we didn't fly every day.

Some days no one flew if the weather was bad. Other days we were given a break in the action. However, this did not mean we were always free to go into Norwich or just to sit around the Officers' Club playing games. Teddy and I were requested to attend a special training course in observation and navigation. We would enter this large room where laid out before us was a small *from Brad Wilson's* STALAG LUFT 1 P.O.W. JOURNAL, 1945

    For a while Don flew "Dixie" and we struggled along with "Barbara"! Oh, what a ship was Barbara! Although this short gruesome narrative deals mainly with the "Dixie Flyer" I don't believe it would be disloyal to mention a few of the struggles we had with "Barbara!"

    "Barbara" was one of the last of her kind to join our group. She wasn't va beautiful shining silver - on the contrary, she was a dull, greasy olive drab. We flew her first with our original crew on one of our early missions. Regardless of the fact that she was nearing antiquity and had chalked up many a mission she was still in excellent shape. The Navigator's compartment was well arranged and comparatively easy to work in - that is if you can consider any B-24 easy to work in.

    One day in early August we took off in Barbara, and she had just had two new engines installed. The engineering office was psychic, for from the time we left the coast of France those two new engines were all we had. One engine had gone out over the target, the other as we hit the Channel. We managed to reach our base with little difficulty. We blessed Barbara! After that she went down to sub-depot for a while and we shifted around from Nita to Silver Dollar to Dixie Flyer and occasionally Weepin' Willie and Wynn With Paige. We were even forced to take Ft. Worth Maid on one mission - a dilapidated relic of days long gone by. She was soon retired as a training ship along with "Nita."

    Around the first of September Teddy and I began to fly with Webster and Sherman and we were re-assigned to Barbara fresh back from sub-depot. But it wasn't the same Barbara. She was changed for the worse! Webster complained that it was all he could do to pull her off the runway - she refused to gain air speed. The navigator's compartment was minus the sling-seat and half the table was irretrievably lost. And Teddy had his own troubles with the bomb racks!

It was a habit of mine to situate myself on the cushioned seat on the flight deck and sort of doze off from engine start until we were airborne, usually twenty minutes to half an hour, but after hearing Web complain about takeoffs resolved to sweat one out. On the morning in question I gazed blissfully out of the flight deck blister at the green grass, oily hardstands, & cold grey sky. The four engines were purring in unison. Barbara buzzed and purred and waddled about the runways, then roared her willingness to be off into the sky as Web revved up the engines. And after the usual delay, throttles were opened and Barbara leaped forward and ran down the runway as tho she were eager to be off but her wings were slightly reluctant. Her nosewheel hugged the runway. I watched the concrete runway slipping past - faster and faster - there couldn't be much runway left but we were still earthbound! Oil stained concrete slipped by in a greyish blur - then suddenly green grass and just a glimmer of light between our wheels and the ground and in ten seconds more then chimney of a house passed under our left wing close enough to reach out and touch. We were airborne, but Barbara used every last inch of runway to do it. We never had the opportunity to try her again. Our next mission was Sept. 12.

scale replica of the German countryside, assembled to scale. It looked much as it might look from the air. Our job was to identify certain targets and "fly" a mission as we walked around the display, keeping close records as we went. It was a rather enjoyable assignment, like a gigantic puzzle to solve. We went at it and accomplished it on short order. We were given other such assignments which we carried out, never realizing that we weren't "ordered" to do this, but were assigned to it, like homework when you are in school. A number of other navigators and pilots were invited to attend these tasks, but they found other things that they had to do. Well, I should have known. After what I had learned in Primary training, you would think I would have been a bit more astute.

7
1944
Barbara

Don, Teddy, Frank, and I, together with our enlisted men, flew 12 missions as a crew. In between we even managed to get another trip into London and several day passes into Norwich. Tibenham was a fairy book village with quaint thatched roof cottages and paths to accommodate more bicyclists than motor cars. We drove through Tibenham each time we went in to Norwich, but never took the time to explore it. There was always tomorrow, we thought then.

Barbara, one of our planes, became an old friend to us. We were assigned to her at least four or five times. She was a big old B-24, painted a dull olive drab, that had seen so many missions that there wasn't room for any more bombs to be painted on her side under the pilot's window. She creaked and groaned and complained a lot as she lumbered through the sky, but she always brought us home again safely. That was more than you could say about the brand new *Dixie Flyer* that couldn't have had more than a half dozen missions on it when it cashed in its chips. But, while *Barbara* looked like she had seen better days, we trusted her especially after our next mission. We flew many different ships, but every now and then, we came back to *Barbara*.

We expected this was going to be a rather routine mission. We were flying to Salzburg to put some munitions plants out of business. Most of the flight would be over France and the flak batteries weren't as concentrated there as they were over Germany. Sure enough, the flight going in was rather routine. We found no opposition all the way to Salzburg. We dropped our payload. Then things started to get different.

I was not aware that our ship had been hit by flak until I looked out the starboard side and saw a feathered prop. Well, I comforted myself, we can make it home on three engines. Then I looked out the port side and there was another feathered prop. Both were, fortunately for us, outboard engines. If you've got to fly a B-24 on two engines, make sure you've got one on each side. Don called me on the intercom and said he couldn't keep up with the group. We were losing air speed. He asked me for a heading—the shortest route back home! Well, this was it! We were over the middle of France and I was on my own. All that time in navigation school had better pay off, now or never! Fortunately, the sky had broken clouds so that I could identify any dominant features on the ground that we passed over. I spread my pilotage

> *from Brad Wilson's* **STALAG LUFT 1 P.O.W. JOURNAL, 1945**
>
> ***Thoughts Concerning Myron Hood Donald:*** *I find it nearly impossible to express in words and most people would never understand how Myron and I always seemed to get a bang out of very little things... commonplace events that with anyone else would have passed without notice assumed an entirely different hue with Myron around. There's the time we were in Norwich together and walked back and forth between two theaters for an hour before deciding which one to go to. Then we sat on the wrong street corner for two hours waiting for the bus back to base! All the time laughing like idiots about little or nothing. And tired old gags we pulled every time we walked along the path to the officers' club. He was more like one of our family than anyone I've ever known. We never knew a serious moment but we understood each other and I knew we could take anything that came along - always laughing. I wonder if I will ever see him again.*

map out on my desk and tried to match what I saw with what was on the map. It worked pretty well when you found a river or a small town that was identified on the map, but most of it was over farmland with no distinguishing characteristics. We struggled on westward and slightly north. By the time we got to the English Channel, we were about halfway between Brest and Cherbourg, opposite the south coast of England with a wide stretch of sea between us.

I started getting position locations from my G-Box. Since the distance was relatively short to England I didn't take time to figure out the wind drift. I just took another G-Box reading and offered Don a course correction in case we were drifting south. This worked pretty well as long as I worked each position location as fast as I could. Finally, we crossed the English coast line, wheels down, trying to look like a crippled ship lest some British gunners think we were a Nazi spy plane trying to look like a B-24 Liberator. We got to a point where we were exactly equidistant from our base and an emergency air field out on the southeast tip of Britain. I told Don and he said, "You decide. Which one do we head for?" Well, we had been flying at a constant altitude for the last half hour and the engines seem to be operating OK. Besides, we were really no closer to one than the other. I looked down at my heavy electric boots and decided I didn't want to walk around in those until we got home. My regular shoes were back at our lockers. It would be a nuisance if we landed out at the emergency field. So I said, "Let's go home." I gave him a heading for our base. Then I looked at the map and noticed the "no fly" zone that extended for several miles in a circle around London. So I computed a slight detour, followed by another G-box reading.

After a few more minutes of pilotage navigation I grabbed my map, disentangled myself from my connections, and went up on the flight deck. "We ought to be over the field soon," I told him. He said, "What's that right down there?" And there it was coming up right under us. We received "instant" landing instructions, and were down in minutes. As we taxied off the runway onto the adjoining tarmac, we could see all these friendly faces, arms waving to us. Our ground crew treated us like royalty! They thought they had lost us. We came to a stop and disembarked. *Barbara* was towed into the hangar for yet another refurbishment. She wasn't done yet, even with some holes in her rudders and damaged wings and two dead engines, *Barbara* would fly again.

When our crew first met in Tucson we were all 2nd Lieutenants. But as soon as we were officially assigned together as a

---

from Brad Wilson's STALAG LUFT 1 P.O.W. JOURNAL, 1945

The Road Not Taken: It was late August when I went to see Captain Kidder, 702nd Squadron Navigator. How different the next year might have been had I accepted his offer at that time. I had just started flying with Webster and Lacey, a navigator with only six missions to go had taken my place with Don. Captain Kidder asked me if I would like to be lead navigator. It sounded good and I asked him if I'd get back with Don's ship when Lacey finished, but he said that Don wasn't scheduled for lead but that I could get back on his crew when Lacey finished in the event that I did not accept lead. So what did bone-head Wilson do? The moron declines lead and all the opportunities that go with it! Its altogether possible that had I accepted that time I wouldn't have had the displeasure of spending the better part of a year in prison camp! I gained nothing in refusing for I never flew again with Don.*

101

> *There was one other incident that brought about my presence in the* Dixie Flyer *on her final mission. Every time it looked as tho I would be taken off Webster's crew that nosey thing called "fate" stuck her finger in my pie and pushed me right back on. It started with Lt. Ralph Shrecke and his co-pilot Lt. August J. Ott. Shrecke was a lead pilot and had gone most of the way to finishing his missions. Then on one unfortunate mission where some fair weather cumulus obscured the target temporarily Shrecke elected not to make a second run on the target whereas other squadrons did. So 1st Lt. Shrecke remained 1st Lt. Shrecke and was relieved of the responsibility of lead pilot. This resulted in a quick reshuffle of deputy-lead crews. Webster was to me made lead and I was to fly with Sollien, another deputy lead, until Lacey finished with Don. But when our next mission came up, the C.Q. called us in the morning and said I was flying with Webster. It seems as tho they decided Webster had too many missions already completed and put a newer crew into lead. So I flew my sixth mission with Web. That was September twelfth.*

* Editor's Note: Actually, my father may have gained quite a lot by his decision. Had he joined the lead plane crew he would likely not have been shot down on September 12th, and instead would still have been flying on September 27, 1944 - just two weeks later - when the infamous Kassel Mission took off. Thirty-seven B-24s of the 445th left Tibenham and only six returned. It was the highest group loss in 8th Air Force history. It is possible that choosing to stay with "his crew" and being subsequently shot down on September 12th saved his life.

crew the first pilot automatically became a 1st Lieutenant. That made him the "crew commander." So when we went overseas, Don was 1st Lieutenant. Not many first pilots made it to Captain right away, but Don did it after only a few missions. Perhaps it had something to do with the way he brought *Barbara* back after she was all shot up and how he handled one landing that could have been disastrous.

We were coming in from one of several missions that had been reasonably flak free and Don was bringing the ship in smooth as always. Frank would often brag to other pilots about his first pilot who brought the plane in with not even a bump as the wheels touched down - every time. And that was a fact. Don was good. Well, on this occasion, he touched down as smooth as usual and

---

LETTER HOME - *August 12, 1944*

Dear Mom 'n Pop,

Remember how I told you I was going to try growing my moustache - again? It has only about eleven hairs (I used a magnifying glass), which is still better than the seven I had last time. I don't know why I tried again so soon.

Theo and I have been taken off Myron's crew - it may be only temporary. They asked me if I'd like to get on a lead crew so I don't know what they'll do for sure. Myron is now a deputy lead, which means he takes over lead of the formation if something happens to the lead in flight. He isn't likely to make actually lead, though, as all of the lead men have about as many missions in as Myron and they'll probably all finish their missions at the same time. At least we're still all in the same barracks. We're just not flying together.

Theo had a baby girl on August 10th. I won the bet!

Bye now,
Brad

then a tire blew. I don't know how he did it, but he guided that plane and slowed it down to a perfect complete stop and pulled it off the runway. Then he radioed in to the tower and they sent out a repair truck. We got in the truck and drove back to the debriefing room as though nothing unusual had happened, while the mechanics changed the tire and towed the plane back to the hangars.

Nobody ever called Don "Myron," (except me, in my letters home, for some reason even I'm not sure of.)   I sort of doubt that his family even did. He was "Don." Back in Tucson we would go out to a local bar for beers and it was Don who first

---

LETTER HOME - *July 28, 1944*

Dear Mom 'n Pop,
 The weather here as usual is spongy. We had a few hot days (with the usual overcast) and then an old fashioned thunderstorm. The distant roar of thunder was quiet compared to the racket of four airplane engines roaring in your ears.
 Speaking of airplanes, I have come to the point where I have a terrific amount of respect for the Liberator (B-24). It's a wonderful ship and it burns me that news accounts of heavy bombardment are being "carried out by so many fortresses"! "Fortresses" strike here! "Fortresses" raid Munich! "Fortresses" bag so many Focke Wulfes! It's disgusting! The Liberators are in there doing as great if not greater jobs than the B-17s! They may not be as streamlined or "dashing" in appearance, but they do a great job. The 24s make a beautiful formation, too. I just wish you could see some of those waves of planes passing over - at times the sky is black with them. A thrilling sight, kids.

Bye now,
Brad

introduced me to pipe smoking. (My parents would have thought I was going to the dogs! Drinking beer and smoking a pipe!) I was smoking a tongue biting "Sir Walter Raleigh" tobacco that had absolutely nothing to offer except a burned tongue. Don suggested an aromatic tobacco that at least smelled good when you lit up. After the first puff, you couldn't smell the aroma anymore, but, I figured other people could and maybe it would make them feel better about the pipe smoke.

Don told the three of us about his sexual exploits in the service and I found these tales rather daring. At one point he told us that he and three other men had lived together with their four girlfriends - all in a single room with four beds crammed in. That seemed a little over the top to me, although I was no prude. I thought it was maybe a tad too public. He laughed, "The noise at night was the sinful part! Who got any sleep?!"

One day just before we shipped out to Lincoln, Nebraska, he got a letter that his folks were coming down on the weekend. Well, that was fine, but they were bringing with them his old girl friend from his home town. That was not good. Don still liked his girl friend from the "live-in" days and he didn't want to start something going again with the girl from home. Besides, he had an idea that she wanted to get married - or engaged, at least - before he went overseas and that wasn't in Don's plans at all. So, they came down and she was all over him and he kept fending her off and finding "duties" he had to do. His parents were no help at all, since they thought she was a "nice girl for Don" and hoped they'd get married some day. He muddled through the weekend and of course, had to go "back to flying on Monday." So they went home, his old girlfriend saddened, but still determined to get him someday.

Looking back on our tour of duty, I realize now that we

had considerable "time off" when we weren't flying missions. Sometimes I personally felt guilty, since those poor guys in the fox holes didn't have the "time off" that we had, and they didn't come home at night after being shot at during the day and have a good meal, a shower, and bunk beds for a good night's rest. There were days when our group wasn't scheduled to fly, there were days when just our crew alone wasn't flying, and there were days when the weather prevented our missions from taking place. We tried to enjoy our time at the base as much as possible. Some days Don and I walked into Norwich, which was not too far. We'd browse through the town, have "fish and chips" at the local restaurant, and just enjoy each other's company. We had established a rapport that was hard to explain to others. We understood each other's sense of humor and we would find laughter in things that to others were just plain nutty. One of the joys of living a long time is that you can look back and remember the good times while all the bad seem to drift away in the haze.

The good times took a back seat to the bad times on my 17th mission, the one from which I wouldn't return. I wasn't with Don and my regular crew for that mission. After I was a POW I thought it was lucky that "my guys" hadn't been there when I was shot down. What I didn't know then - but I soon learned -was that Don, Frank Smith, and the rest of my crew faced their own disaster shortly after mine.

It was after our next trip to London that we returned to find that two of us had been temporarily reassigned to Webster's crew. No one ever explained why the reassignment was made. Teddy and I were just told to report with Webster's crew for the next mission. We wondered if it had anything to do with the special "training assignments" that we had recently completed with flying colors.

As I mentioned before, Web had a reputation for being reckless, and we had enough problems with the enemy without worrying about a reckless pilot. However, ours was not to reason why, and the brass wanted me to report with Webster's crew. So Teddy and I hoisted ourselves and our equipment onto Webster's plane. The next four flights went reasonably well, with no heavy opposition from the enemy. There were targets where the flak was heavy, but it was always two or three thousand feet below us, just puffs of black smoke that looked thick enough to get out and walk on. The German gunners just didn't have our altitude dialed in. Web behaved rather well and didn't get into any trouble. We didn't have much time to socialize with the new crew since we were flying missions on a fairly tight schedule.

One morning we were not assigned a mission and I was called to the Commanding Officer's Office. This was very unusual. I had never had any contact with the Colonel before and wondered what I had done now. I was sent into his office, stood there at attention and saluted. The Colonel said, "Lieutenant, would you like to consider taking an appointment as lead navigator? This would mean some additional training and, of course, a promotion." I had been on four missions with Webster, and I had no idea who I'd be flying with as lead navigator. I asked the Colonel "Is my old crew being considered for lead ship also?" He said, no, they are not. I didn't even take a moment to think it over. I said, "If it would be possible, I would prefer being reassigned back to my old crew." He said he completely understood, and he guaranteed I would be back with my old crew after our next mission. It's strange, but the camaraderie of flying with your old team meant more than promotions, prestige, or whatever else came from being in the lead ship. That was considered reason enough by the brass, and I would be back with Don and company after my next mission. Later, I decided that the work we had done on our special assignments must have influenced them to make this offer. I never had a chance to ask Teddy if he was approached to become lead bombardier. The next day, things got a little hectic.

8
1944
Prisoner Of War

The *Dixie Flyer* was possibly the newest ship I had ever flown in, aside from the factory-fresh plane I flew to Europe in. It was not painted olive-drab like the old ships were. It was shiny aluminum with the name *Dixie Flyer* emblazoned on the nose in bright red and yellow. I have a feeling that if I had been in *Barbara* that day we might have missed getting hit by that flak. *Barbara* led a charmed life.

from Brad Wilson's STALAG LUFT 1 P.O.W. JOURNAL, 1945

September 12, 1944

That is the day my number came up, you could say. Certainly none of us on the crew ever anticipated such events. It couldn't happen to us! It only happened to the other guys. But we were the guys who always came back. We didn't qualify that with the additional words "so far." After several days in which absolutely nothing changed my new reality came upon me with amazing rapidity.

On September 11 we didn't fly. It was one of those drab listless days at the base - no letters, nothing different. We'd seen the movie "Double Indemnity" the night before and didn't want to go see it again. Don and I went to the PX to get our weekly rations of candy, gum, cookies, soap, razor blades and so forth. We got a great bang out of some new routine we'd worked up on the way over - we were always on some senseless doubletalk routine that never developed into anything very hilarious except to us. We went back to the hut to pick up "F.C." & "Theo" for dinner, but as usual "F.C." was sleeping and insisted on prolonging this occupation for at least the time being. So Theo, Myron and I went to dinner and then to the Club to write letters.

It was a little after two A.M.

The next morning when we were called for briefing they didn't wake Don & Smith. Theo and I were flying with Webster again - it was a surprise to me. We ate a light breakfast of powdered egg omelette, grapefruit juice, bread, butter & jam. Then we dashed down to the briefing room as usual. We were scheduled for the Dixie Flyer. Our mission wasn't anything out of the ordinary. In fact, it wasn't as long as most of them. The greatest part of our course was over the North Sea, then south between Heligoland and the North Frisian Islands, thence slightly westward to Hannover and out over the Zuider Zee and back to England. The main briefing over, I went to the navigator's briefing and then to the dressing room and on out to the ship for the inevitable wait. The usual amount of "tenseness" prevailed. Webster was asleep on the cot in the engineers' tent. Sherman, Theo, Shaver, Brennan and I were stretched out on the hardstand, the rest of the boys were asleep in the waist of the ship. The light of the new day was getting stronger. The yellow and red nose wheel of the Dixie Flyer assumed its natural hues out of the grey overtones of the early morning twilight. On an adjoining hardstand they were running up the engines of a "24." Then they were cut off and silence cloaked the entire field - the silence before my storm.

I was dozing peacefully when Web's bulk loomed over me. He stretched and yawned to Sherman, "Get the boys together, Jack. It's almost time to start." Before we went on each mission we held a brief powow with the enlisted men giving them general information on where we were going and what to expect in the way of enemy resistance. How little we knew of what was in store for us in that category - a brief volley from a four gun battery when we had survived seventy times that number and come back unscathed! C'est le guerre!

The calm morning air lost its tranquility and began to vibrate harshly with the pulsating reverberations of hundreds of engines and whirling props. The Dixie Flyer moved slowly from the hardstand, Slowly forward dipping and nodding and groaning and squeaking, protestations at the appliance of the brakes, out along the endless perimeter track to the takeoff positions. A short delay here as Web revs up each engine to 2700 RPM. Then move up again as other planes take off ahead of you and finally the Dixir Flyer sidles into position and throttles are opened. A great force seems to be holding you back as the ship moves forward, accelerating rapidly. The runway is clear. Wheels are coming up. The patchwork English landscape below you is taking shape and becoming clear as you gain altitude. You keep climbing and begin to circle the Buncher; the assembly has begun.

I began having trouble early that morning. The mike switch began to stick just after we had left the Buncher. At first it just required a little persuasion and tapping to keep it working, but in a matter of a few minutes it ceased operation altogether and I switched to the bombardier's lines with the same result. The mike switch on that line was out altogether. Despite feverish manipulation not even a click was audible over my headset.

So the somewhat annoying - to say the least - situation existed that I could hear everything said over interphone but I couldn't contact anyone! I wrote Teddy a note and slipped it to him in the nose turret whereby he would contact Web for me over his mike each time I gave him a note with data or interrogations.

About eight o'clock that morning we left the English coast for the last time on a combat mission. Our squadron was flying with another group that day which led me to believe that he who flies with anyone but his own group has had it right from the start.

We headed out over the North Sea from Cromer and at the [strikeout] the wing assembly point had managed to get ten miles off the briefed course.

The sky was clear for the most part until we reached a point approx abeam of Emden. From that point on eastward there was a solid undercast. We continued to head north and at last G Fix were forty miles north of our briefed route. About the time I had decided the whole wing was going to Sweden the lead ships turned south southwest and we were headed for our briefed turning point some 52 miles away. Up to this time it had succeeded in being a very unpleasant mission but I seriously underestimated its possibilities when I ventured the opinion to myself that it couldn't get much worse.

I glanced out a side blister and below us there extended an endless ocean of greyish white stratus and above us cirro-stratus. My ETA for intersection with our briefed course near the briefed turning point was up and we were still heading SSW instead of SSE.

It was time for another D.R. position entry in my log and I had just begun to fill in the required data when the ship gave a sudden lurch as tho caught in some heavy prop wash. Many things that take quite a lot of time to tell about here happened then in split seconds.

I didn't realize immediately that anything serious had occurred but almost simultaneously with the lurch Web's voice *came over the interphone, "Grab her, Jack, I think I'm blacking out!" An instant later the turret doors hit my back and Teddy tumbled down into my compartment. He was unhurt but his face as he ripped off the oxygen mask was a bluish white. He hollered in my ear and pointed out the window. There was a dead prop on the port side - No. 1 engine was pockmarked with flak holes. At the same time I heard Web, who had managed to hold onto his consciousness, hollering "Brad, can I salvo? Give me a heading! Brad! Why don't you answer?" Under the strain and stress he overlooked the fact that my mike switch was out. I pulled my mike cord out and plugged into the turret connection and pressed the mike button, but connections there had been damaged by the flak. I turned back with Web's semi-hysterical voice in my ears. Teddy was sitting on the floor with his oxygen mask plugged back in. All of my instruments were out. The altimeter still read 22,500. I wrote Web a note telling him to salvo and take a heading of 270 degrees. The Danish peninsula lay between us and Sweden and with solid undercast and all our instruments out there was little chance of us crossing such a large area without contacting at least one or two flak batteries.*

Teddy took the note up to Web using the walk around bottle. I took a look at my mercator, grabbed it off the desk, and said to hell with the oxygen and went up on the flight deck where I could get the facts of the situation!

Dixie took the hit and started a downward glide that would end in a field on an island in the North Frisian group. In all its silvery beauty, it plunged earthward and crashed ignominiously east of where we were rounded up.

After pulling my chest parachute out manually, I landed hard on my feet and crushed a disk in my spine. We were all quickly surrounded by German soldiers. It took me many minutes to regain my breath, all the time at gunpoint.

We sat in the middle of that Field on Ameland Island all day, with the soldiers guarding us, with nothing to eat or drink. After a couple of hours I felt I really needed to relieve my bowels. They were still working on my regular schedule and with all the unexpected excitement they told me it was time to GO now! Here I was - injured, behind enemy lines, with enemy guns pointed at my head - and all I could think about was getting a chance to pee. I told the little German guard who had first greeted me in English that I needed to go. He understood quite well, and he took me over to a small outhouse. He didn't trust me alone, so he peeked in every now and then to make sure I wasn't hatching some diabolical plan to escape. I sat there, perhaps a bit longer than I needed to. I thought, well, I won't be eating very well for a long time, so enjoy this elimination process while you can. Soon there won't be anything to eliminate. And that was closer to the truth than I realized.

When I came out, he happily escorted me back to our small circle and then started talking to us. According to his story he was from Kansas. He had emigrated to the US in the late '20's, moved

---

from Brad Wilson's STALAG LUFT 1 P.O.W. JOURNAL, 1945

We left by train in the morning. The train was crowded. We had the privilege pf compartments - ten men to a six place compartment. Everyone was exchanging sad stories. The phrase

> "sad story" eventually became "Horror Story." but it was still too early for that. The crash of the "Dixie Flyer" was quite commonplace among the horror stories and lacked some of the more vivid characteristics of others. But to us it was real and vivid enough and held all the horror of combat that any of us would ever care to encounter.
>
> We arrived at the transient camp at Wetzler on September 26 and there we had our first taste of Red Cross Food. It was delicious. Sherman was a great help to me for at the time I didn't get around too well and air raids were a dime a dozen. we had to make for the shelters day or night whenever the sirens blew. I met Ralph Hogan there in a shelter during a raid and you'd have thought we were life long buddies! We discussed everyone we'd ever known, where they were, what they were doing. We left for Barth on the thirteenth. We spent four days on the train in the same crowded condition with a half Red Cross box a piece to live on. It was a happy day when we arrived at Barth for what we thought would be a short stay.

to Kansas, and was doing quite well there until just before the war when he came home to Germany to visit his family. As soon as he got home he was drafted. So now he was a soldier in the Luftwaffe. He didn't appear to be bitter about it but, of course, there were other soldiers within hearing and he probably wouldn't have wanted them to hear if he was upset with the Fatherland.

It was dusk before we moved out. All this time we weren't allowed to talk to each other. The Germans said "Nein!" We wondered where Teddy was and the three gunners from the waist and tail turret. They had not shown up during the day. Finally, some other soldiers appeared and we were marched across this large field toward a farmhouse. There we saw a road and we were taken down it to a dock where we boarded a small launch that carried us across the water to the mainland.

Once on shore, we were marched through the small town to their city jail. This was the first time we really felt like prisoners. We were ushered into cells where we discovered a number of other Allied airmen who had been rounded up during the day. It made us feel a bit better to see we were not alone. This sort of thing did happen to others, too. Jack Sherman and I talked for the first time about the experience. The first question we all had was what happened to Teddy and the three gunners? I told him that the last I saw of Teddy he was heading back to the bomb bay to rig for possible water landing. When we went to bail out, since there was no intercom working, Sherman had sent the radio man back to the waist of the ship but no one was there. The only thing we could assume is that they hadn't waited for the order to bail out and had jumped early while we were still over the North Sea. If so, the water was too cold to survive in more than twenty minutes and they were lost. We hoped we might see them in the groups of prisoners that were being added to our cells, but we never saw them again.

The next morning, we marched outside to board a wood-burning bus that would drive us to the train station. Once there, we boarded a train which already had several hundred prisoners on board. What had happened the day before? It seemed like we could have no air force left with all the crews bailing out over Holland. The train pulled out and headed south. Late in the day we pulled into a large marshaling yard in a city in the Netherlands. There some German Officers came through the train and my pilot, Web, and I were taken off the train. We were taken to a hospital somewhere and each of us was put in separate rooms. A doctor in uniform came in and spoke to me in German. I just shook my head and indicated I didn't understand. They X-rayed my back and left me lying on an examination table all night. I was worried now that I would never see the rest of my crew again and we'd end up in different prison camps. I had no idea why they were examining me. My back hurt, but I could walk. Web was taken somewhere else to have his legs inspected since they were pockmarked with flak. Once during the night the German doctor came in with my X-rays, looked at them, and muttered to an attendant in English, "Poor devil." What? What? Why was I a poor devil? What was the matter with me? I never knew until I got home a year later.

At dawn Web and I were taken out and returned to the train station where the train was still waiting. The cars had been side-tracked and now they were adding more cars to the train. Soon after we were back on board and the train started rolling and continued its southerly route through the Netherlands and Belgium. About mid morning the train stopped again in a large station. Here a group of Nuns brought food to the train. We hadn't eaten in almost 48 hours and whatever they had we'd gratefully accept. They brought us small bowls of mashed potatoes and green beans - delicious! It wasn't much, but it did give our stomachs something to work on. That was our feast for the day.

Sometime, perhaps approaching midnight, the train pulled into a large marshaling yard and stopped. The sign on the station identified it as Koln, also known as Cologne, depending on who it belonged to at the time. We were deep in the Ruhr Valley, a prime target for the RAF almost any night. While we sat there, we heard an air raid siren and then the distant rumble of bombers coming toward us. The German guards came through the cars and moved us out as quickly as they could into an air raid shelter beneath the railroad station. There were so many of us that we were packed in there solidly, standing room only. We had just gotten into the shelter when the "all clear" sounded and we were marshaled back onto the train. Cologne wasn't the RAF target that night.

Trying to sleep on the train was not too easy. First, my mind kept dwelling on my predicament - specifically what my injury might mean for how the Germans treated me. We were wedged into the seats, three men sitting in a normal seat for two. Add to that the frequent stopping and starting of the train, the rumbling of my empty stomach, the guards going up and down the aisles with their rifles in hand, and sleeping became a precious commodity not easily come by. Finally, through sheer exhaustion, I eventually dropped off to sleep sporadically.

The train headed east, and with each passing clickety-clack our hopes grew fainter that we would be able to escape and find our way back to the coast. England and the allies were in the other direction. We passed through some pretty hills covered with apple orchards, stopping occasionally at small towns. It would have been pleasant if I had been a tourist. After one stop at a small town, the guards came through our car, one carrying a loaf of bread and a long stick of bologna and a knife. The other followed directly behind him with his rifle at the ready, in case anyone tried to overpower the guard with the knife. The first guard deftly sliced off a piece of bologna and a piece of bread and gave each prisoner his meal for the day.

The trip seemed like it would last forever. Then one morning the train pulled into another large marshaling yard that looked like it had been repeatedly bombed but was currently in reasonable repair. We were in Frankfurt-on-Main. (The name was to differentiate the city from Frankfurt-on-Oder further east). This had been a big industrial city. Now it was in shambles. We were herded off the train, formed into long lines, and marched down one of the main streets. The streets were lined with the shells of tall buildings that had been bombed repeatedly. Their outer walls still stood; the windows were just holes and the were interiors gutted. The streets were also lined with local citizens who took a distinct

---

from Brad Wilson's STALAG LUFT 1 P.O.W. JOURNAL, 1945

I was led to an office that was small and stuffy. The walls were covered with pictures of B-17s and 24s, the desk littered with folders and papers concerning Groups, Wings and Divisions of the Eighth Air force. But the room was warm - at least warmer than the solitary confinement of our cells. I'd been here once before - just seven days before. He'd asked me questions then concerning our plane and squadron, target and so forth. He wasn't at all pleased with the answers. So for one week I waited in my cell - no one summoned me - nothing happened except bread twice a day and soup once a day. Now I was back in the room again and he was smiling. He knew the answers now.

Among the papers on the desk I saw the name "Dixie Flyer" written with various notations pertaining to that ship and its last flight.

The interrogator was explaining that the Dixie Flyer had not burned but had crashed in he shallows off the SE coast of Ameland. He told me my squadron number, Group personnel at the group & a few other things that he though interesting. He also mentioned that Teddy had been found in the plane - I didn't say anything but I didn't believe him, then.

I shaved that afternoon for the first time in over two weeks and that evening I was taken from my cell to a nearby barracks where Sherman, Shaver, Brennan and I were once more re-united. That was a great night of rejoicing. After eight days and nights of solitary confinement we reveled in the great luxury

> *of companionship once again. Talk of food was predominant and it was on this evening that we first made the acquaintance of F/O Raymond Rudolph, Glider Pilot, adventurer, and narrator of tales both tall & short. Rudolph as in heaven as long as he had someone to bend an ear to him. And on this nite he monopolized conversation with various menus a la Rudolph that he would have when he got back to the states.*

dislike to us immediately! They started throwing things at us; whatever they could get their hands on, and shouted curses at us in German. This was not a pleasant march, and it went on all the way across the city to the small town of Wetzlar on the outskirts. Here there was a transient camp for POW's and we were marched in behind the first barbed wire enclosures we had seen thus far.

No sooner had we been assigned to barracks than the air raid siren blew and we were marched out into an air raid shelter. Frankfurt was still a target for the USAAF and air raid sirens were frequent. When the all-clear siren blew we walked out of the underground bunker and I saw a face that looked familiar. It was so out-of-place that it took me a few moments to recognize Ralph Hogan, my old high school classmate from Ukiah who I had last seen on my trip to San Francisco! That one moment did wonders for my attitude. Here, in this horrible place was a friendly face! Not just anyone... someone from home. It was an instant reminder that somewhere out there home still existed. Ralph and I started trading war stories and filled each other in on our wartime adventures. Shortly, though, like our first day in the Army when we were separated by our train departures, we were again separated. Ralph had been at the transient camp for a while and was now due to be shipped out to a permanent camp somewhere. I never saw Ralph again during the war, although I suspect he was among the

5000 men who were sent to Stalag Luft 1, which is where I was headed.

We ate in a mess hall. The food was served by other prisoners like us. The quantity of the food was small, but it tasted like ambrosia from the gods. Hot food, served on plates! Here we finally got to talking to each other. This had not been allowed on the train, with the exception of whatever occasional mumbling we could get away with. It was easy to learn any man's life history. Just ask him a question and he started babbling and would keep going for hours if you didn't stop him. Everybody wanted to talk. John Felding, who was sitting next to me at the table one day, said, "Watch Grayson." Grayson was sitting across the table from us and down a few seats. "He's an only child in his family—you can spot them every time." The servers were dishing up the food on the plates in the middle of the table. When they finished, each man would grab a plate. Well, Grayson had his eyes glued on the operation and when he saw a dish that he thought had a little more food on it than the others, he threw his fork into the midst of it to "stake it out" as his. Felding said, "See! He does it every time." I agreed with him, but I didn't tell him I was an "only child" and didn't go around "staking out" my plate each meal. I think there was more to it than the fact that Grayson was an only child. Maybe he was just really hungry!

We were at the Wetzlar Transient Camp for a few days. More prisoners were coming in regularly. While we were here each man was issued a Red Cross POW package that contained a tooth brush, a razor, a comb, and we were given our own "US" Army blanket and a pair of "US" Army shoes—all furnished through the Red Cross and shipped in from Sweden. With this we also got a duffel bag of sorts. We had belongings again! The electric boots that we had been wearing since we were shot down were confiscated. So were my two wrist watches - one my own, the other a government issue for navigational purposes. I had one handkerchief which had to suffice. I got a cold while at Wetzlar and I was constantly washing out that one handkerchief and trying to dry it before I needed it again for my next "blow."

We weren't looking forward to our march through town again to catch the train to only god-knows-where. Luckily the return march didn't draw the attention that our arrival had. Finally one morning we were told to form a line once again, duffel bags hanging over our shoulders, and out we went. The train hadn't improved any. Once again we were wedged into our seats, only now with the added baggage to make room for. Our train moved out, continuing east, and we wondered how long it would be until we met the Russians coming the other direction.

On the next to last day of our train trip we turned in a northerly direction. Late that night we were once again stopped in a huge marshaling yard. We couldn't immediately identify the city, but later, as the train moved on, we passed a station that said, "Berlin." While we were sitting there, with only the gentle sound of men breathing (occasionally snoring), there was a sudden explosive sound, repeated three times. Every man must have jumped a foot. It seems as though a lone British Mosquito night bomber was on his way home from his assignment and dropped down into the Berlin marshaling yard to strafe some target of opportunity. Apparently, he took our train as that target, since it was not identified as a POW conveyance. We never knew if his quick strafe did any damage, but no prisoners were hurt and the train pulled out soon thereafter.

The train pulled into a small town about 100 miles north of Berlin. The sign on the station read "Barth." We were herded

U.S. Air Force photo
A B-24, hit by enemy flak and going down.

Brad Wilson, age 1 (1922) with his Aunt Elsie

Brad in 1939 at age 18

Brad's mother, Lenoir, in 1925

The "Big House" in Almaden

August and Emily Zeiler, Brad's grandparents, around 1880.

Lenoir & Lee "L.B." Wilson, Brad's parents, around 1960

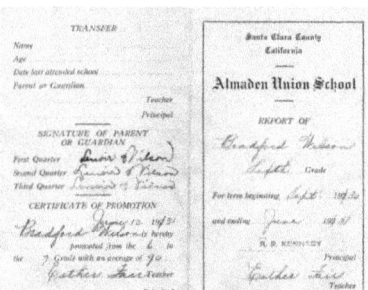

A report card from Almaden in 1931

Ukiah, California

Brad joins the United States Army Air Force

Brad and his grandmother Emily during his leave before shipping overseas. This is the last photograph of them taken together.

Brad showing off his dress uniform during leave.

126

Brad in his "Aviator's finest" and, below, the same photo from his training class graduation book. The "nickname" shall go unexplained!

Bradford Perry Wilson
Ukiah, California
"Tripod"

Ryan PT-22, a two-seat open cockpit trainer used during World War II
U.S. Air Force photo

Stearman PT-17
Photo courtesy Juergen Lehle (albspotter.eu)

AT-7 Navigator Training Plane
U.S. Air Force photo

B-24 Liberator
U.S. Air Force photo

B-24 nose turret

Norden bombsight

The *Dixie Flyer* herself, before she crashed into the North Sea

Artwork based on U.S. Air Force photo

A squadron of B-24s headed out on a bombing run.

U.S. Air Force photo

U.S. Air Force photo

Bombs away.

U.S. Air Force photo

and headed home.

The *Dixie Flyer* ready to go; her last mission would be September 12, 1944

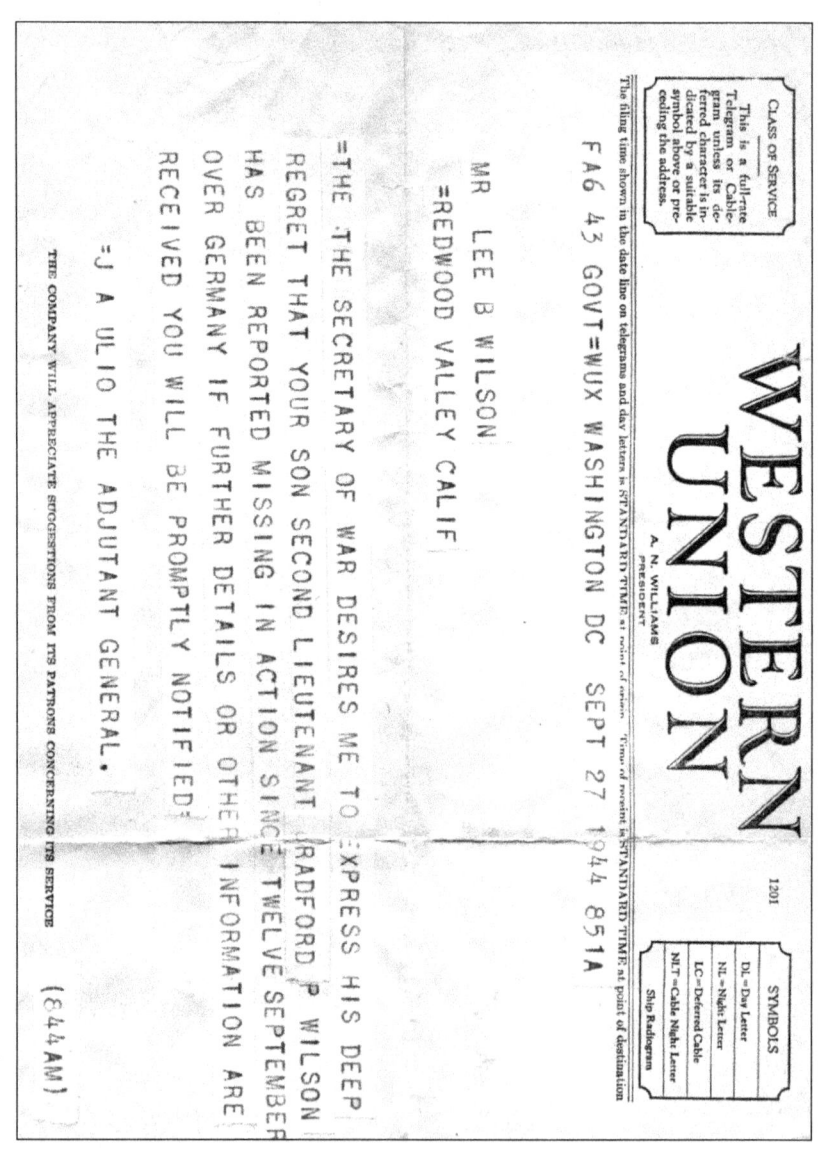

"Western Union Telegram, September 27, 1944:
THE SECRETARY OF WAR DESIRES ME TO EXPRESS HIS DEEP REGRET THAT YOUR SON SECOND LIEUTENANT BRADFORD P. WILSON HAS BEEN REPORTED MISSING IN ACTION SINCE TWELVE SEPTEMBER OVER GERMANY. IF FURTHER DETAILS OR OTHER INFORMATION ARE RECEIVED YOU WILL BE PROMPTLY NOTIFIED."

```
                                                                    mlj
                          WAR DEPARTMENT
                      THE ADJUTANT GENERAL'S OFFICE
IN REPLY REFER TO:         WASHINGTON 25, D. C.
AG 201 Wilson, Bradford P.
PC-N ETO 196
                                                      28 September 1944
```

Mr. Lee B. Wilson

Redwood Valley, California

Dear Mr. Wilson:

     This letter is to confirm my recent telegram in which you were regretfully informed that your son, Second Lieutenant Bradford P. Wilson, 0713032, Air Corps, has been reported missing in action over Germany since 12 September 1944.

     I know that added distress is caused by failure to receive more information or details. Therefore, I wish to assure you that at any time additional information is received it will be transmitted to you without delay, and, if in the meantime no additional information is received, I will again communicate with you at the expiration of three months. Also, it is the policy of the Commanding General of the Army Air Forces upon receipt of the "Missing Air Crew Report" to convey to you any details that might be contained in that report.

     The term "missing in action" is used only to indicate that the whereabouts or status of an individual is not immediately known. It is not intended to convey the impression that the case is closed. I wish to emphasize that every effort is exerted continuously to clear up the status of our personnel. Under war conditions this is a difficult task as you must readily realize. Experience has shown that many persons reported missing in action are subsequently reported as prisoners of war, but as this information is furnished by countries with which we are at war, the War Department is helpless to expedite such reports. However, in order to relieve financial worry, Congress has enacted legislation which continues in force the pay, allowances and allotments to dependents of personnel being carried in a missing status.

     Permit me to extend to you my heartfelt sympathy during this period of uncertainty.

                                          Sincerely yours,

                                          J. A. ULIO
                                          Major General,
                                         The Adjutant General.

A War Department letter that followed the initial telegram by a day

ADDRESS REPLY TO
COMMANDING GENERAL, ARMY AIR FORCES
WASHINGTON 25, D. C.

ATTENTION: AFPPA-8

HEADQUARTERS, ARMY AIR FORCES
WASHINGTON

AAF 201 - (8922) Wilson, Bradford P.
0713032

October 26, 1944.

Mr. Lee B. Wilson,
Redwood Valley,
California.

Dear Mr. Wilson:

    I am writing you with reference to your son, Second Lieutenant Bradford P. Wilson, who was reported by The Adjutant General as missing in action over Germany since September 12th.

    Further information dated September 14th has just been received which indicates that Lieutenant Wilson was a crew member of a B-24 (Liberator) bomber which participated in a bombardment mission over Germany on September 12th. Details are not available, but the report indicates that during this mission at about 10:30 a.m., near Heligoland, Germany, your son's plane sustained damage from enemy antiaircraft fire, and when last observed was disappearing into an undercast, under control but losing altitude rapidly. The crew members of planes returning from this mission were unable to furnish any other details relative to the circumstances surrounding the loss of this aircraft.

    Due to necessity for military security, it is regretted that the names of those who were in the plane and the names and addresses of their next of kin may not be furnished at the present time.

    Please be assured that a continuing search by land, sea, and air is being made to discover the whereabouts of our missing personnel. As our armies advance over enemy occupied territory, special troops are assigned to this task, and all agencies of the government in every country are constantly sending in details which aid us in bringing additional information to you.

Very sincerely,

E. A. Bradunas

E. A. BRADUNAS,
Major, A. G. D.,
Chief, Notification Branch,
Personal Affairs Division,
Assistant Chief of Air Staff, Personnel.

A War Department letter dated one month later, October 26th. Still no news whether Brad was alive or dead.

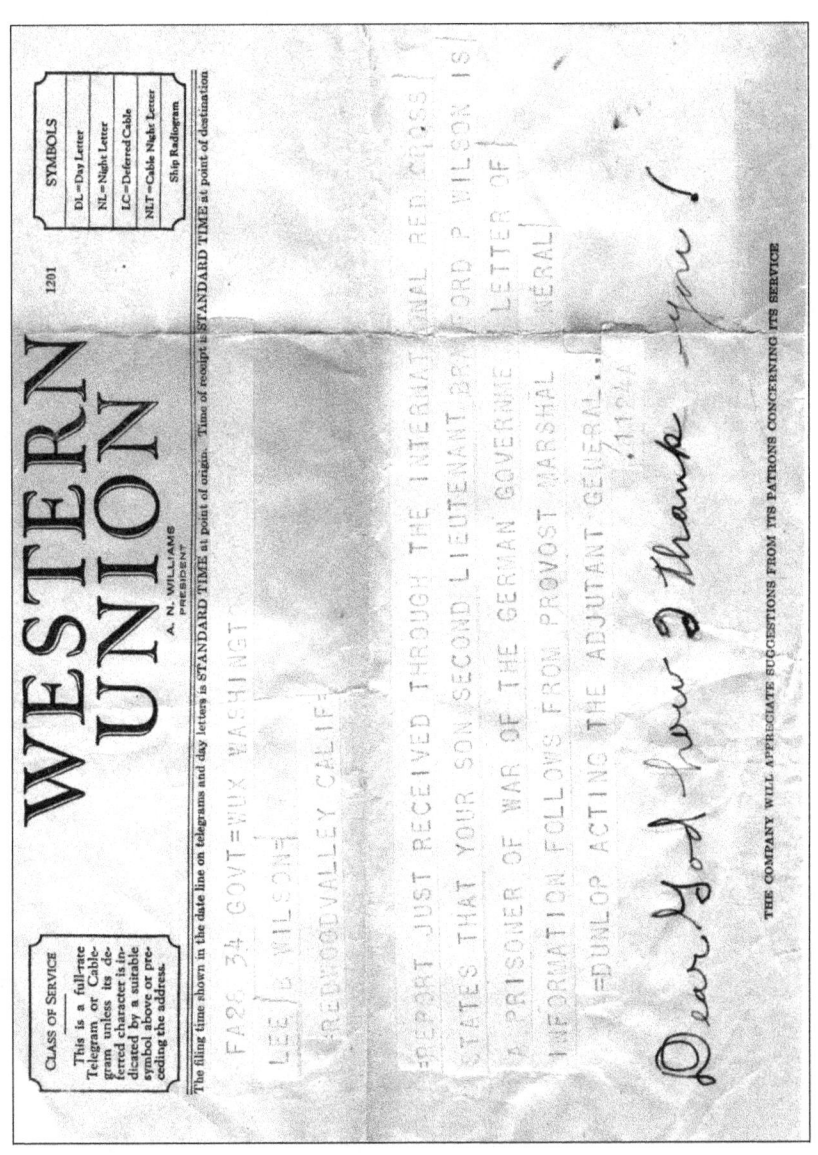

Western Union Telegram, December 27, 1944:
REPORT RECEIVED THROUGH INTERNATIONAL RED CROSS. STATES THAT YOUR SON SECOND LIEUTENANT BRADFORD P. WILSON IS A PRISONER OF WAR OF THE GERMAN GOVERNMENT. LETTER OF INFORMATION FOLLOWS FROM PROVOST MARSHAL GENERAL.

Pilot Kenneth Webster,
who was in charge of the
Dixie Flyer when it went down

Photo courtesy Roy Kilminster, RAF POW

POWs marched through Barth, Germany

The first notice Brad's parents got in his own hand that he was still alive, three months after he was reported missing.

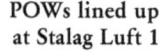

Arriving by Train in Barth

Photo by Heinrich Haslob, German guard

POWs lined up at Stalag Luft 1

Photo courtesy Dana Harding, daughter of William J. Harding

 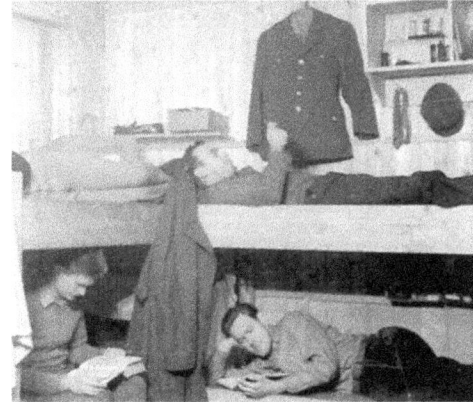

There wasn't much to do besides read, play games and sleep. The occasional play or boxing match was put on when approved by their captors, but on a daily basis this was life in Stalag Luft 1.

Roll call

Photo courtesy Randy Anderson, USAAF Navigator

The "TTT" above this stage, arranged in the mess hall, signified another production of the "Table Top Thespians"

A SAMPLE RED CROSS PARCEL

- CORNED BEEF
- POWDERED MILK
- OLEOMARGARINE
- CIGARETTES
- SALMON
- PORK LUNCH MEAT
- BISCUITS
- RAISINS
- LIVER PASTE
- CHEESE
- SOAP
- ORANGE CONCENTRATE
- COFFEE
- CHOCOLATE
- SUGAR

Based on a photo from "Behind Barbed Wire" by Morris J. Roy

Photo courtesy Randy Anderson, USAAF Navigator
A barracks stove - for heating and cooking

Photo courtesy Randy Anderson, USAAF Navigator
A guard tower

Photo courtesy Dana Harding, daughter of William J. Harding
The German command at Stalag Luft 1

Photo courtesy Dana Harding, daughter of William J. Harding
A guard tower covered in snow

Stalag Luft 1

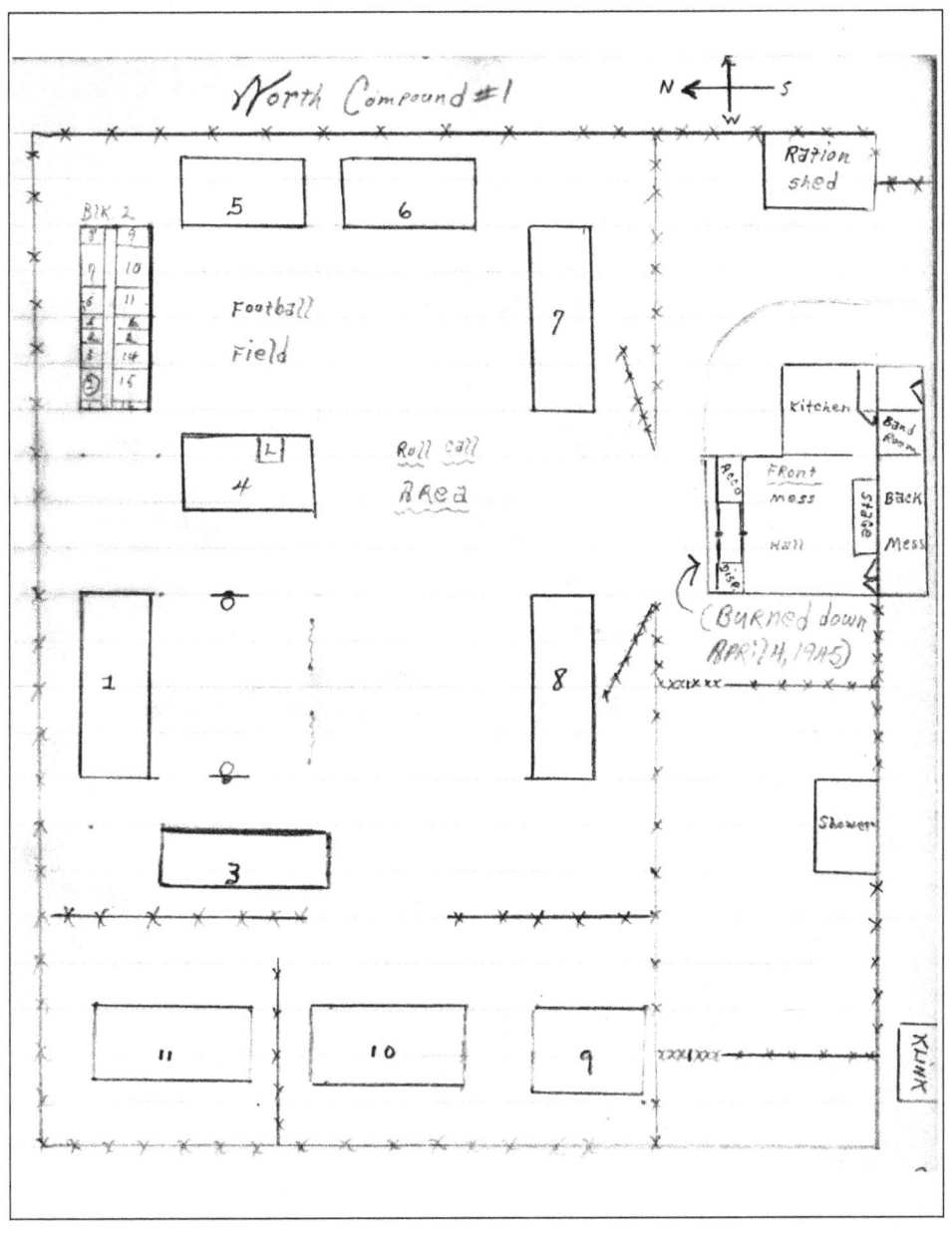

from Brad Wilson's POW Journal -
A map of the North Compound 1

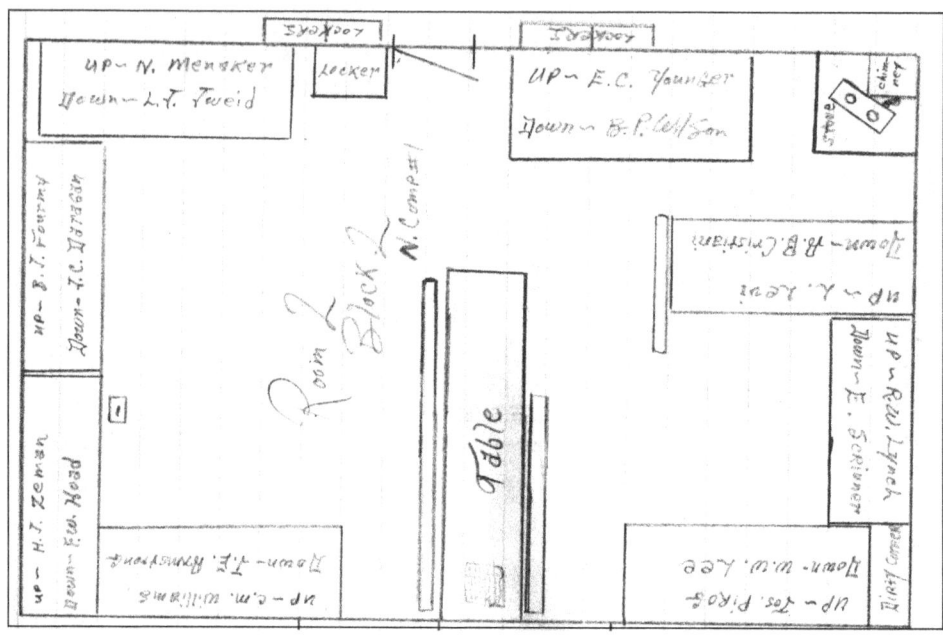

from Brad Wilson's POW Journal -
A map of Room 11, Block (Barracks) 9 in the West Compound 2

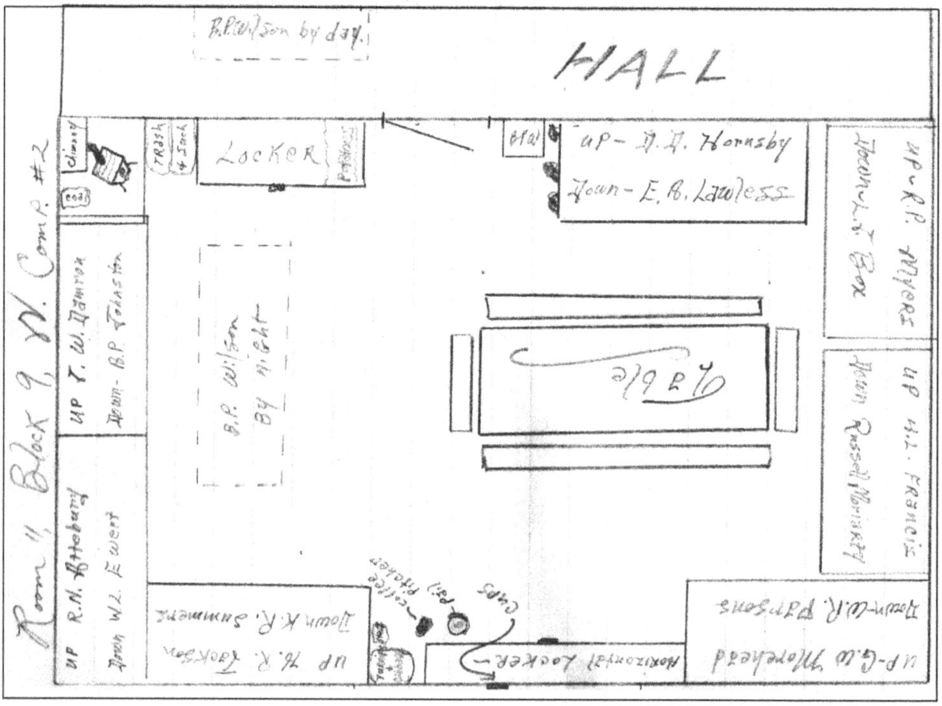

from Brad Wilson's POW Journal -
A map of Room 2, Block (Barracks) 2 in the North Compound

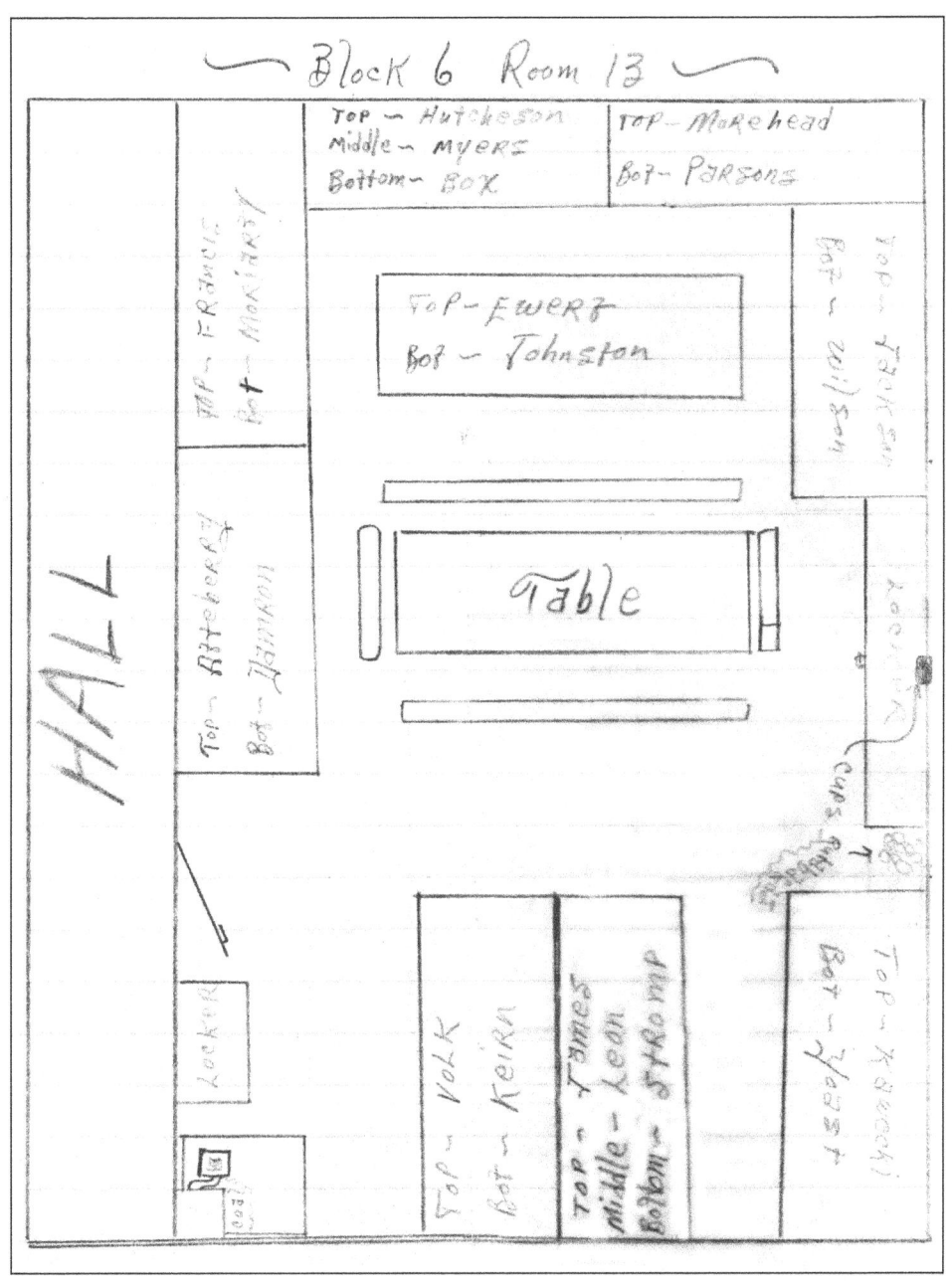

from Brad Wilson's POW Journal -
A map of Room 13, Block (Barracks) 6

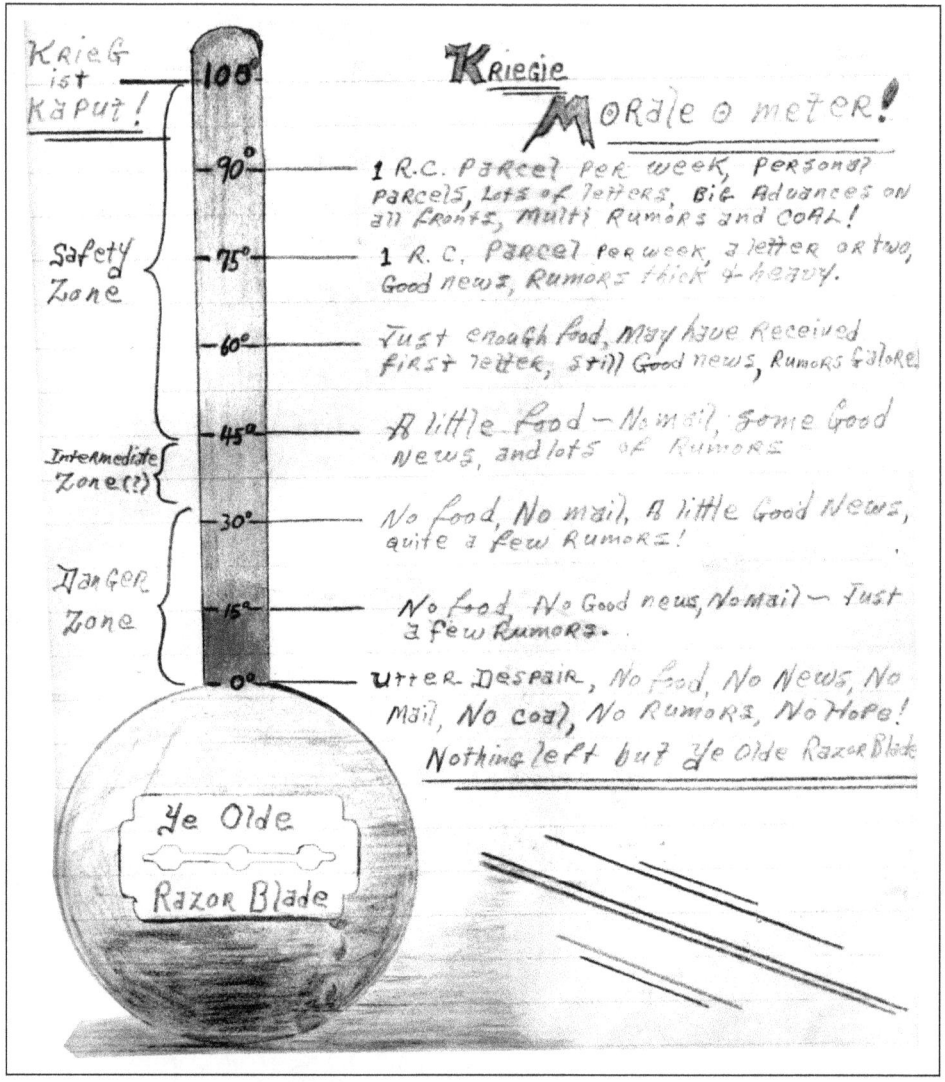

from Brad Wilson's POW Journal -
The Krigie Morale-o-Meter

Morale-o-tures for Months at Stalag					
	Nov 1 to 16	77°	Jan 1-19	70°	Mar 12-26	45°
	Nov 16-30	73°	Jan 19-31	73°	Mar 27	85°
	Dec 1-15	73°	Feb 1-21	72°	Mar 27- Apr 29	87°
Sept. (Oberüsel) 5°-8°	Dec 15-23	74°	Feb 21-28	60°	April 30, 1945	103°!
Sept. (Dulag) 40°	Dec 23	79°	Mar 1-12	35°		
Oct. (Stalag) 75°	Dec 23-31	75°	(famine)			

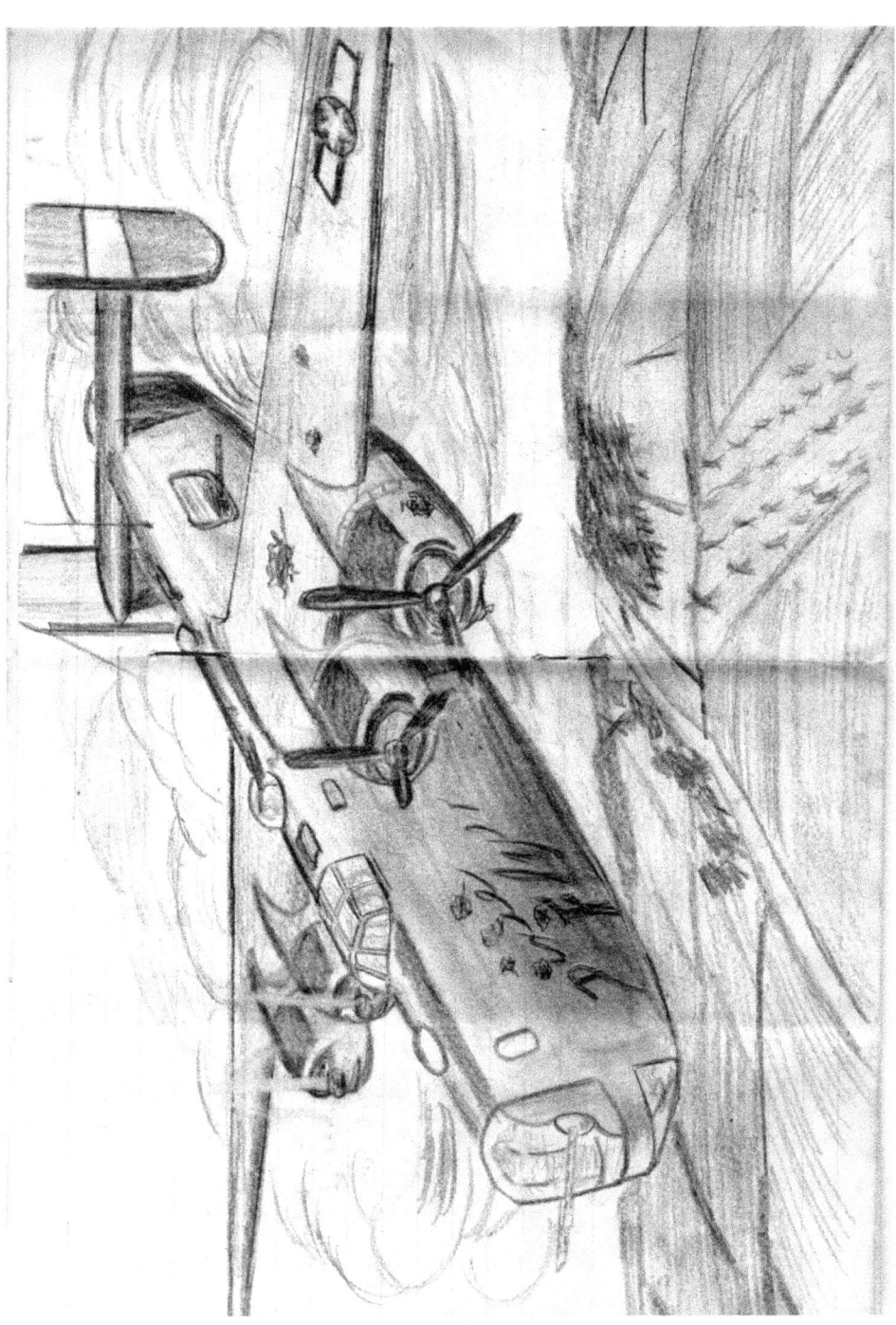

from Brad Wilson's POW Journal -
A sketch of the *Dixie Flyer*

Brad and Joy Wilson on their wedding day. They celebrated their fifty-ninth anniversary on July 10, 2007.

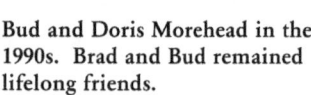

Bud and Doris Morehead in the 1990s. Brad and Bud remained lifelong friends.

Left to right: Brad Wilson, Joy Wilson, Doris Morehead & Bud Morehead in the late 1940s. Bud was Brad's roommate at Stalag Luft 1.

Brad's family in the 1960s; Wife Joy, cousin Virginia Huber, and Brad (rear, left to right), and his kids Crystal, Perry and Brook (front, left to right)

Brad Wilson, circa 1980s

Brad and his granddaughter Alexandria, taken in 2006.

Brad in November, 2007, one week before his death, having a splendid time at a family Thanksgiving celebration.

Brad's family around 1994, left to right:
Joy Wilson, Brook Wilson, Perry Wilson, Crystal Wilson Breazeale, Jessica Breazeale, Robert Breazeale, Orpha Frerichs (Joy's mother), and Brad

off the train again, formed into marching lines, and started tramping in a northerly direction. There were no crowds here throwing rocks at us, just a few curious bystanders. After about a half an hour we arrived at barbed wire enclosures. This was the Kriegsgefangenenlager Stalag Luft 1A, which would be my home for the next eight months. Groups of us were ushered into a very large room where we were seated in one big circle. A jug of water was passed around and we all drank as much as we could from it before it was grabbed away by the next dried out prisoner. A group of German Officers took turns haranguing us in German about what we were doing to their country. Since I didn't understand very much German it sounded very fierce and threatening. This went on for some time until they started leading us away one at a time and put us in individual isolation cells. These cells were about eight by ten feet with insulated walls so that I could hear little or nothing that was going on outside. Each contained only a cot for sleeping and had one small, high window with opaque glass criss-crossed with wire. This was my home for the next eight days.

    Solitary confinement was something I had never anticipated or experienced. The next eight days were probably the longest of my life. In the morning, the door was unlocked and I was given brot and tea. In the evening, a guard repeated the procedure, giving me cabbage soup and tea. The tea was made from rose leaves and had a bitter taste. The diet is to be highly recommended for anyone who really wants to lose weight. If I needed to use the toilet, I had to pound on the door and wait for a guard to come and escort me to the toilet down the hall. I began looking forward to those short excursions. They were a brief break from the monotony. There was little to see except a long hall with doors all along both sides, but I did at least get to see the guard - a real live human being - for a few brief moments. The guards never

> *from Brad Wilson's* STALAG LUFT 1 P.O.W. JOURNAL
>
> *We hadn't been at Barth too long when I saw Ira Weinstein and learned for the first time of the Kassel raid of September 24 when our group lost more than thirty planes. I learned, however, that "F.C." was in a hospital somewhere and that Don was dead. Don and Teddy. Stidham had cleared the plane, but Kielar, McEntee, Modlin, Walston - all had presumably crashed with the ship. How short a time before had we been training together and laughing together and generally enjoying life...*

talked to me. They just took me to the toilet and back.

I found two interesting pursuits to keep me busy while I was incarcerated. First, the mattress on the cot was the home to a colony of fleas who immediately took up residence in my clothes, feeding on my body as their needs arose. So, with nothing but time on my hands, I went through the process at least twice a day of taking off all my clothes, and catching and killing as many fleas as I could get my hands on. I did the same to the mattress and as the week progressed there were actually fewer fleas to kill each time I went through the process. After that exercise I would pace back and forth in my cell, trying to tire myself out for a good night's sleep. There was nothing worse than lying in bed in the dark and letting my mind dwell on unpleasant possibilities while I fought to get to sleep. Lastly, I would engage in my review of the "Hit Parade." I was an avid listener to that radio program before the war and I had memorized every hit song for the past five years or more. I would sing as loudly as I could - every hit song I knew - going from one to another until I had run out of songs in my repertoire. Then

I started over. This went on until I finally got hoarse. Then I would go back to killing fleas or pacing. It helped move the time along.

We had no idea how many days we would be in solitary but finally on the eighth day a guard came in and took me out to see yet another German Officer. This one spoke clear English and started the process of interrogating me. We had been briefed on the pitfalls of answering questions in such an interrogation, so we were to give only our name, rank and serial number. The Officer didn't like that at all. He kept on questioning me for at least a half an hour, lecturing to me about how the Germans already had all the information that I could possibly give them anyway, so I might as well "fess up" to whatever he wanted me to confess. When I didn't, he finally called the guard and had me taken to a large room with walls lined with bunks two to three high. The room was teaming with prisoners like me who had been isolated for the last eight days. An English airman told me, "I saw them taking you out of the room next to mine. I heard you singing in your cell. Very brave. Stout heart! Keep it up!" He went on and joined the others. I didn't realize I was "being brave." I was just singing to help pass the time. Well, I'm glad it made him happy!

We spent that night sleeping in this bunk room. I don't know how many men were in there. The room was packed with GI's all jabbering away at once. After a week's isolation, everybody wanted to talk at the same time and no one was listening to anything else that was being said. The big problem was that every airman there had gone through what must have been the most traumatic experience of his life, beginning with being shot down, and no one else wanted to hear about it! Each man had a similar story, which he considered far more traumatic than the other guy's.

Back in training or at the Air Base, whenever you got a

> *from Brad Wilson's* STALAG LUFT 1 P.O.W. JOURNAL
>
> **JANUARY 20, 1945**
>
> *I lived in the North Compound #1 until January 19, 1945 (yesterday). I've now moved to North Compound #2 In North-one Friday was "Happy Red Cross Day" for a long while. In North-two the day varied from week to week. Here we cook in our own room in a 15 man combine with frequent cakes and pies made by Chief Chef Hornsby assisted by Asst. Chef Morehead. I am starting this journal (which I have titled "The Saga of The Dixie Flyer - A Horror Story in One Volume!") because I finally have enough paper to do so!*

bunch of GI's together the main topic of conversation generally turned to women and sex. But once we got to prison camp that changed. After the initial unloading of stories about being shot down, the conversation always turned to a single subject; FOOD. That's all any of us could think about. We tortured ourselves with visions of our favorite foods, which we wouldn't see again until the war was over. Then we tortured our buddies with descriptions of menus at our favorite restaurants; rare steak, mashed potatoes, ice cream! Finally we talked ourselves to sleep and awoke the next morning to find ourselves being marched out again to one of the five compounds that made up the camp.

  I ended up in Compound One. Together with a glider pilot I was placed in a room with twenty other POWs. At first we were treated as German spies by our fellow prisoners, since it was a policy not to accept any new men "into the fold" until they had time to check them out. In theory, it was anticipated that the Germans would infiltrate the POW camp with spies who would try to pick up scraps of information from prisoners which might be of help to the German war effort. It took about two to three weeks for us to be "checked out" thoroughly enough that the rest of the Kriegies, as we now referred to ourselves, would accept us as genuine. In the meantime, we still wanted to tell somebody all about that fateful day when we were shot down, but no one was interested. This was very frustrating, to say the least!

We were allowed to write home once a week. We received one piece of paper per week that when folded properly made its own envelope. This mail was properly censored by the Germans before it went out. This caused, of course, serious delays in getting the letters to the Red Cross for delivery. I arrived home in California a year later before any of my letters arrived. I was actually home and got the mail myself the day they all arrived in one huge bundle! However, months earlier and not knowing that my letters would be so terribly delayed, I faithfully wrote home each week and told my folks everything was fine. I was healthy and unhurt. Probably the worst feeling is not for yourself, but for your family that doesn't know what happened to you. That was my biggest worry from the day I was shot down.

My grandmother, Emily, was 86 when I went into the Army. She was, to me, the sweetest, kindest person I had ever known. We were always very close. When I lived at home in Redwood Valley, I walked up to my Aunt Bebe's home where Emily lived almost every day. Sometimes she was there alone; sometimes Bebe was there, too. Either way, the first thing Emily did was march me into the kitchen and prepare me some lunch. No matter that I had only recently eaten, she had to fix something for me. And she always had something for me to take home. We talked for hours and she was always alert and interested in everything that was going on in my life. It was exceptionally hard for me not knowing

> **LETTER HOME** - *October 15, 1944*
> *(received February 12, 1945)*
>
> *Dear Folks,*
> *I hope you have heard from the army by now and know that I'm all right. As long as you folks don't worry everything is OK. It's just a matter of waiting until the war is over and then we'll all be together again. We have plenty of clothes and some good food by the courtesy of the American Red Cross, which is my favorite organization from now on. It will probably take ages for you to get this, but write to me if you deem it advisable. You'll know what's best. Take good care of Emily and you take good care of Noan, Pop. I hope we'll be celebrating my next birthday together.*
>
> *Bye for now,*
> *Brad*
>
> [Emily had passed by the time this letter was received. Brad was still in Stalag Luft 1 on his next birthday, which was just two days after his parents finally received the letter. – Ed.]

how she was holding up with the bad news from the war. Those weekly letters that I sent home were mostly addressed to her, telling her to pass on what good news I had to the rest of the family. As the months went by and there was no mail from home, I had a strong premonition that she would no longer be there when I returned.

At some point in time the Army followed up my "MIA" telegram with another that told my family that I was listed as a prisoner of war. We had no way of knowing how soon this would happen, but we hoped the family knew at least in a couple of months. That period of doubt ate away at my insides, along with the clay-like substance that passed for bread in our diet. We got two pieces of "brot" each day per Kriegie. Later, we learned that the brot was made up of 60% flour and 40% sawdust. I also found out, much to my dismay, that eating it "raw" as it was sliced off the loaf was a disaster for your stomach. It had to be toasted first to make it edible. I learned that just a bit too late. With the constant concern about my family and the raw bread, I developed a duodenal ulcer. I couldn't eat for about a week. When I resumed eating, I toasted my bread each day, like all the other Kriegies. This was accomplished by laying the bread on the top of a 1-square foot stove top until it browned. The stove was fueled by coal bricks, of which we were allotted seven per day. This was to keep us warm and allow us to cook occasionally.

About two weeks after my arrival in Compound One I saw Ira Weinstein. Ira was a navigator in the 445th Bomb Group and took my place with my old crew when I was transferred to Webster's ship. I was walking around the perimeter of our compound when I saw this familiar face over in the next compound. I stopped to welcome him to our illustrious camp. Standing well back from the barbed wire that separated us so as not to antagonize the guards, we talked for some time.

This was the first I had heard about the disastrous Kassel Mission in which the 445th was almost wiped out. It was flown just about two weeks after we had been shot down. On the morning of that mission, thirty-six B-24's from our group took off for Kassel, Germany. Of those thirty-six only three returned. They were hit by the elusive Messerschmitts and Focke-Wulfe fighters that we had never seen on any of our 17 missions. It was after their bomb run and they were returning to England, unfortunately without their fighter escort who had gone off to strafe other enemy targets, when the German fighters descended on them. The whole battle lasted little more than five minutes, barely enough time for the fighter escort to return to the scene and clear the air of the enemy fighters. And in that short time thirty-three ships went down. Weinstein had bailed out of his ship though the nose door, some members went out the bomb bay, but Don kept the ship going to the last minute and only had time to go out the top hatch behind the pilot's seat. This was a dangerous exit, since the B-24's horizontal stabilizers could easily hit you as the plane plunged downward. Weinstein thought that Don's legs were hit as he plunged head-first downward. When he landed, he didn't move and Weinstein saw an irate German farmer come up to Don's inert body and plunge a pitchfork through him several times. That was possibly the worst moment of the war for me.

Frank Smith, my old co-pilot, had survived and I met him later when I was transferred to Compound Two. Jack Sherman, my co-pilot on Webster's crew was also in that compound. I never saw Webster again for 55 years, and then discovered him in 1999 on the Internet!

The food that kept us alive was furnished mainly through Red Cross parcels. We were supposed to get one package per man per week. However, the Germans told us that they were unable to deliver that many packages each week. They were brought in from Sweden by ship to the nearest port and then transported by truck to the various prison camps. When the war was "going well" for them, we usually got a full package per week. But whenever they received some stunning reverses (which was most of the time), they cut back on the total packages.

In each package was a can of Spam, a can of Klim (Borden's powdered milk), a package of raisins or prunes, a chocolate "D-bar" (a very hard milk chocolate concoction from Hershey), a half-pound package of sugar, instant coffee, 2 packages of cigarettes, a package of "K-ration" crackers (a sort of very heavy graham cracker) and a small can of fruit preserve.

During my stay in Compound One we all ate our dinner in a mess hall. The food was prepared by our own POWs from whatever the Germans allowed us that week, plus the rations from the Red Cross Parcels. When the parcels came in they went directly to the mess hall. There they would take out the Spam and the Klim, and then distribute the rest of the package to each man. The remaining food in the packages was used by us for breakfast or for snacks for as long as it lasted. The raisins were highly prized over

---

from Brad Wilson's STALAG LUFT 1 P.O.W. JOURNAL

FEBRUARY 20, 1945

On Thanksgiving Day 1944 the Mess Hall gave out canned roast beef that they had been saving for the occasion - plus raisin pie. Levi and Feldman did a couple of impersonations and the band played on! But other than a few days like this - Christmas, New Year's, etc., there is very little to distinguish one day from another. Roll call, breakfast, lunch, roll call, dinner - day in and day out. And because of this lack of diversified living, strange tho it may seem, days pass with unusual rapidity and at the time of this writing it hardly seems possible that six months have passed as a P.O.W.!

Many snowfalls have come and gone during the winter, but on the whole the weather has been fairly mild. On Feb. 19 we received some sergeants in our compound moved here from a POW camp on the east front. Our camp has received several lots of POWs from the east in the past month, raising our population from about 5000 to 8000.

the prunes and became a "high cost" bargaining item. Also, the cigarettes were good for bargaining if you didn't smoke them yourself. We had chain smokers who would go berserk by the end of the week when they ran out of cigarettes.

When our parcels were reduced to 4/5 of a parcel per Kriegie, it became a bit more difficult to divide up some of the items. Each room had a "captain" who was in charge of how we set up our distribution system. He had to have the Wisdom of Solomon to settle any disputes. Since everyone now didn't get one of each there was a lot of trading and bartering going on. An "Acco" was set up in the compound where accounts were kept regarding who "deposited" food and who "withdrew" another. If I had a package of raisins I was willing to part with, I could turn them in and get 100 points. I might withdraw a chocolate D-bar for 60 points and have 40 left over for my next "purchase". There was one commodity that garnered no points whatsoever; Orange Marmalade. Any kind of berry preserve, or even peach or apricot was acceptable. But you could hardly give away orange marmalade.

That Christmas the Red Cross provided special holiday packages. Instead of Spam we got canned turkey. In addition, each parcel contained a "gift" of some sort, such as a pipe, a package of pipe tobacco, a wash cloth, a tiny chess set, etc. These arrived during the 4/5ths package per man era. So once again care had to be taken in dividing things up fairly.

Our mess hall served a dual purpose. At one end was a stage and we had thespians among the prisoners who put on "Broadway" productions at least twice during the months that I was in Compound One. The Red Cross also furnished us with musical instruments, a variety of costumes, and the books on plays. One of the big productions I recall was "The Man Who Came To

Dinner." Of course, men had to play both the male and female roles, but they were made up and costumed so well we had a hard time believing they weren't women. We also had some "stand-up" comedians that were as good as any I'd ever seen back home. The Army Air Corps was, after all, was made up of a cross section of American life, and had many young men who either were or would become professional performers. Unfortunately all these good things came to an end.

In the mess hall we had a map on the wall with pins and strings delineating where the war front was at that time. This line was established as a result of the word given us from the Germans, so we couldn't be too sure of its authenticity. One day after the Battle of the Bulge had begun the map was updated, and the lines

---

LETTER HOME - *November 9, 1944*
(received February 26, 1945)

Dear Folks,

I am gradually becoming a veteran Kriegie – which is how they refer to a prisoner of war. Mail from home is coming in daily, so I hope to get a letter from you folks by sometime in December. My address is Stalag Luft 1 via Stalag Luft 3 and my prison number 5966. At any rate, I know you have heard from me by now and know everything is OK. Frank Smith from Oakland is here now, too. I haven't heard about Myron, though. I remember in my last letter to you before I became a prisoner I gave you Theo's wife's address. I hope you have written to her as she would probably appreciate a little morale building right now what with little Elzie and all. Well, folks, more soon – love and kisses

Bye now,
Brad

> **LETTER HOME** - *November 9, 1944*
> *(received February 19, 1945)*
>
> *Dear Folks,*
> *Here it is nearly Thanksgiving and the weather isn't very cold as yet. We have a biting wind now and then but it warms up as soon as the wind dies down. Even though we aren't all together I have lots to be thankful for. I'm alive and well and looking forward to the Great day when our little family can be together again. I hope Frank Smith and I get to travel home together. If Myron and Theo were with us it would really be a great day. Meanwhile, I'm still hoping I might get a letter from you. I want you folks to take good care of yourselves and work up good appetites, because when I get home we are going to have some fancy meals to make up for lost time - believe me!*
>
> *Bye now,*
> *Brad*

that had looked like we were making reasonable progress suddenly moved west again in... well, a big bulge. Unfortunately we got the news from BBC over a radio we had smuggled into camp that the Allied withdrawal was true. For a while, it looked like the Germans would press right on to the English Channel once again. Before long, luckily, they ran out of fuel for their vehicles. They began moving guns and munitions by horse and wagon and the advance came to a halt.

Three days after Christmas - for reasons unknown to any of us - a number of us Kriegies were reassigned to other compounds. I was moved to Compound Two. There were a total of 5 compounds in the camp. Here I joined a room with 26 other Kriegies. Our bunks were stacked three high. At first my bunk was placed out in the hall and my "cardboard box" - the place where I kept the few personal items I had collected in the past few months - was hung up on the wall next to the door. Every night just before lights-out, we had to drag my bed in from the hall, since the guards didn't allow anyone to sleep in the halls. Then in the morning, after roll call, we'd drag it back out again to give us room to move in the cramped area.

To add to this confusion there was no mess hall in this compound. All the food was prepared in our own rooms on the tiny stove I mentioned before. We had "cooks" who had volunteered to prepare the "main course," whatever that might be. Usually, that was cooked cabbage, potatoes, or yellow turnips. They would do strange things with the Spam and turn it into some kind of gravy. When you are hungry you'll eat just about anything.

Just two weeks after I moved to Compound Two we had a big fire in the camp. The mess hall in Compound One burned to the ground. I figured I got out of there just in the nick of time. The Kriegies in that compound now had no way to prepare their foods, other than eating it raw. Since the men in Compound Two had been making their own food for a while they had experience in this unique art. They had cooking utensils (made by the Kriegies themselves) and had some sort of organization to the food preparation. I never found out how they fared in making the transition to "barracks cooking" over in Compound One.

Eventually I volunteered to become a "baker." Now you might ask what I could possibly bake with the ingredients we were given. The powdered milk we received in our Red Cross parcels came in the "old reliable" Klim cans. These held one pound of dry milk. The ever ingenious Yankees decided to use them to make bigger cooking pots. Using a table knife (which we were allowed,

157

> **LETTER HOME** - *December 12, 1944*
> *(received February 19, 1945)*
>
> *Dear Folks,*
> *December is now progressing and we have had only one flurry of snow which promptly melted and mild foggy days have taken over. I suspect we'll be in for colder weather as winter approaches, but we are prepared. Seeing as I likely won't be able to make it home for my birthday this letter will have to take its place. But by the time another year rolls around I expect we'll be celebrating such events together again and will have more or less forgotten all these we've missed. You've no doubt heard from the Red Cross about sending packages and so forth. I don't know how long they take to get here, but if you have figured I'd ever get one you've probably sent one by now. The most important thing I need is a letter! Am expecting one soon!*
>
> *Bye for now,*
> *Brad*

along with forks and spoons) the knife was sharpened as much as possible on a stone from the yard. Then this knife was used to cut the can down the side and around the bottom by pounding on it with a rock, another knife handle, or whatever instrument we came up with. This, then, gave us a flat piece of tin. By crimping the edge over and inserting it into a crimped edge from another can and then beating them down flat and tight, we could make bigger and bigger pieces of flat tin. To make the seal tighter, a nail was removed from a table in our room and was used as a punch to beat down on the seam. After getting enough pieces put together that way, they were folded into rectangular pans and the corners were again beat down till they were tight. If it was done right this resulted in a water-tight container. We had lots of these pans on hand to bake and cook in. Of course, we had no oven. So the ever-resourceful Kriegies built one to sit on top of our small stove. It could also serve as a toaster. If we'd had just had a slightly larger stove and a few more bricks of coa we would have been set, but we made-do with what we had.

In Compound Two one of my new roommates was a guy named Bud Morehead. Bud and I clicked right away and we stayed very close friends for the next fifty-four years, until his death in 1998. He never lived very far from our homes (we moved around quite a bit, but always within a few hours of Sacramento, California, where Bud and his wife Doris lived.) He attended the Davis campus of the University of California after the war and stayed in the Sacramento area for his whole career. Our families often went camping together, visited each other, and later when we both retired we traveled to Mexico together.

But as the New Year dawned in Stalag Luft 1A we weren't looking forward to those future days. One cold day in January Bud and I decided to bake a cake for dessert! We thought that might cheer up the guys. The question was how we could do that out of our meager rations? We decided that the room's stash of groceries included sufficient K-ration crackers, sugar, chocolate d-bars, powdered milk, and raisins to make one. We grated up the d-bars on a Kriegie grater (a perforated piece of tin) to make powdered chocolate, and did the same to the crackers to make flour. We mixed this together with sugar, powdered milk, raisins and some water, smoothed it out in the pan, and baked it in the Kriegie oven. Of course we had no baking powder to help it rise, so it came out rather flat. But as I remember it now, sixty years later, it is still the best tasting cake I ever ate. Everyone in our room had a piece of that cake for dinner and loved it.

Among our other discoveries were Kriegie almonds.

Someone discovered that if you broke open a prune pit there was a small nut inside that resembled an almond. If you roasted it for a while you ended up with a very tasty nut. There wasn't anything that was edible (or that could be rendered edible) that got away from us. During snow storms some Kriegies would go out and gather up fresh snow, mix it with powdered milk and sugar and have a "snow cones."

from Brad Wilson's STALAG LUFT 1 P.O.W. JOURNAL

MARCH 8, 1945

Feb. 19th was the last time we had lights at night - a few weeks previous to that the lights came on and went off at sporadic intervals every evening. On March 7 a loudspeaker was installed in our barracks and we now hear the German radio during the day and evening.

9
1945
The Long Wait

The move to Compound Two was followed by the long wait. Despite the fact that it was winter and the length of time between sunrise and sunset was rather short, the days kept getting longer and longer. To keep up some semblance of a healthy routine, we walked around the compound twenty or thirty laps to tire ourselves out so that could sleep at night. During the first days after I arrived our senior officers called us out for calisthenics. But due to poor nutrition that was soon discontinued. Many of the prisoners were too weak to keep up with strenuous exercise.

Our bunks consisted of one inch by four inch slats which supported a huge burlap sack of wood shavings. These shavings packed down fairly quickly and at least once every day we had to take the sack out and "fluff it up." Our fun-loving Kriegies liked to play tricks on each other, and occasionally they'd come up with something really sadistic. In our room some of the bunks were stacked three high. That meant that you couldn't sit up in your bunk very easily and the top man had just enough room to roll into his bunk because the ceiling was just inches above him. One day the fellow from the top bunk was out on a walk and some of his friends decided to "fix" his bunk. They pried the runners that supported the slats apart just enough to grab onto the end of the slats and keep them from falling. That night, he climbed the edges of the lower bunks and threw himself onto his mattress which promptly descended with him onto the man underneath, whose slats also collapsed and fell on the man in the bottom bunk, with all three hitting the floor. I don't think any of the three guys involved were particularly happy. At least they weren't laughing.

But most of the others who were "in on the action" thought it was hilarious.

Bed slats provided many wonderful hobbies for some of the gifted Kriegies. One man, in particular, was willing to give up some of his slats, (which made the bed more uncomfortable, since the mattress would sag between the remaining slats), just so that he could use the wood to make a violin. He had made musical instruments before the war. Once again, the common table knife was used as the main tool. With more patience than I could ever conceive he worked for at least two years - cutting, scraping and shaping the wood. From the table we had in the room he scraped excess glue that had oozed out from the joints, and found a way to use it to glue his work of art together. He managed to get strings through the Red Cross and he finished it before the war ended. Amazingly, it looked and sounded as good as any violin I had ever seen. Human beings are capable of some wonderful things, even in the most adverse conditions (maybe especially in those conditions.)

Some of the activities weren't quite in the same cultural category. But they used up time that hung heavy on our hands. One of the first men I'd met in camp was a fellow named Hennessey. He was rather serious, read a lot, and was comparatively quiet. So I was quite amazed one day when I came in from my walk to see him lying flat on his back with his pants down, his legs back over his head and his bare bottom pointed skyward. He had quite a gathering around him and one man standing there with a box of matches, poised, ready to strike. "OK," Hennessey said, "Here comes one!" So as the guy with the matches struck one and held it close to Hennessey's bottom, Hennessey let one rip and a blue flame about three inches long shot out of his bottom. All the guys were laughing and Hennessey *from Brad Wilson's* STALAG LUFT 1 P.O.W. JOURNAL

MARCH 10, 1945

On March 9, just to contradict my statement above, the Germans turned on the lights for one hour - from 8pm to 9pm. This may or may not become a regular feature. News continues to be good - it won't be long now, will it? No mail! Not much hopes either.

said, "That's the last one! That one burned all the hair off my ass!" And they all laughed harder. It seems as though someone else's discomfort, whatever it was, was cause for laughter, whether it was having two beds collapsing with two men in them, or burning all the hair off someone's ass! I asked Hennessey later what brought that activity on and he said, "Oh we used to do that all the time in Boy Scouts." I never knew what cultural activities I missed by not being a Boy Scout!

One day I was walking around the compound with Hennessey and I asked him about another prisoner named Moriarty. He was a handsome Irishman, except for the three teeth he was missing. He was very quiet, kept to himself, never smiled and didn't partake in any activities with the other Kriegies. Hennessey said, "Well, he's got a lot to worry him. It seems as though when Moriarty was shot down over France he managed to evade capture. He was on his own, wandering the French countryside for several days before being found by the French Resistance. They took him in, fed him, got him civilian clothes, and were preparing to ship him out and get him back to England. In the resistance he met a young girl with whom he fell in love -

from Brad Wilson's STALAG LUFT 1 P.O.W. JOURNAL

MARCH 12, 1945

Our last Red Cross issue was ¼ box per man the third week of Feb. None since - up to this time, March 12, 1945. Dried vegetables, potatoes, rutabagas, sugar, bread, and occasional cooked meat, barley and margarine are keeping us going. Then there is a small ration of ersatz coffee, too, but no need to mention that!

sounds like a movie, but this is the truth! Well, she was assigned to smuggle him out to the coast and they were well on their way when they were discovered by the Gestapo. Being in civilian clothes, he was treated as a spy. They took him in and questioned him over and over again, beating him and knocking out those missing teeth you've noticed. Eventually, they decided he was just a British airman and they turned him over to the Luftwaffe. They in turn ended up sending him here to Stalagluft 1A. Meanwhile, what had happened to the girl? Moriarty never knew and it's been eating at him ever since. He feels responsible for getting her in that situation, which really could have happened to her at any time, being in the Resistance. So he has a deep hatred for the Germans and won't talk about what happened to anyone. I may be the only person he ever revealed this to."

This story has a more bizarre ending. When the Germans finally left Stalag 1A we were told to stay in camp and await the arrival of the 8th Air Force to fly us out. Well, some guys had been there just a little too long and were stir-crazy, so they disobeyed and left, heading south and west over the German countryside.

Moriarty was one of them. More than a year later I heard from another prisoner from our room who had headed out at the same time. He told me that Moriarty got to France and headed for the same village where he had been befriended by the Resistance. There he searched for news on what had happened to the girl. Unbelievably, she had gotten away and was unharmed. Moriarty reported to his superiors, got their permission, and went back to the village, married the girl and stayed in France. There aren't many war stories that have an ending like that.

Without the help of the Red Cross we would have been in bad shape. Among the things that they managed to ship to us through Sweden were books. These were mostly British novels of adventure and intrigue. But they helped pass the time. There was one novel I recall in particular called "Norman Conquest." It was not about the real Norman Conquest in the year 1066, but about some adventurer named Norman Conquest who went around righting wrongs and being a good guy - doing in the bad guys left and right. He was sort of like a latter day Robin Hood or Zorro, or perhaps an early day super hero, who always left his trademark behind - "1066" - scrawled on the scene much the same way Zorro left his "Z." My biggest problem with this book was that Norman would get into the worst possible situations where no living being could possibly extricate himself and there he would be left, in cliffhanger fashion, at the end of the chapter! Then the next chapter would begin and he would be completely out of trouble, with no explanation how he managed the feat! Sort of like an old Saturday afternoon serial at the movies where they left the hero in dire straits, only to have him pop right out the next week in top condition, ready to take on the villain again!

We were allowed showers about once a month. On those occasions the men in each room in turn were given so many minutes in a big room lined with shower heads. If you were lucky, the water was warm. We were given soap and told to get with it! Each shower lasted only about five minutes, so there wasn't much time for scrubbing. We were in and out of there, dried off and dressed within 10 minutes. We had our own towels (we had picked up at Wetzlar via the Red Cross). We were responsible for washing our own socks and underwear, of course, and that was rather difficult, since we didn't have any spares. We could have used some.

Another thing we could have used more of was paper. Any kind of writing paper. At some point in my stay at Stalag 1A we were given a composition book, like we used to get in school once in a while. There were highly prized. I wrote down thoughts in this book and then a few days later, to save paper, I would carefully erase the whole page and start over again. I like to write humorous

from Brad Wilson's STALAG LUFT 1 P.O.W. JOURNAL

MARCH 17, 1945

Moving day! Wheels and Germans conspired to make unpleasant conditions still more unpleasant. Our room has moved to Block Six, Room 13. A stove about 15 inches square on top serves to cook food for twenty men! What a life! Patton is barely keeping our hopes up with his spectacular drives. Bread now coming from Barth may stop at any time and we'll have to bake our own - only God knows how! The coal suypply is supposed to last until about the middle of April. On the night of March 18 a heavy fog sent some ducks crashing into a barracks - one flew in an open window! The result - Roast Duck!

poetry and I had much grist for the mill in this camp. So I started writing poems about Kriegie life. One was titled, "Johnny Comes Home" and told the tale of what parents, wives, and friends might expect from an ex-POW when he got home. Other Kriegies read my poems and found them interesting enough that they copied them down in their books. Another rather lengthy poem was titled "The Germans Called it 'Brot.'" It was also copied by other Kriegies and some months later when I was waiting shipment home in a camp in France, I found that poem was being distributed by the Red Cross with a by-line reading: "Anon"! That was my poem and I didn't even get a by-line!

I also copied a number of poems that others had written. One of my favorites was a simple little four line stanza that read:

As I wished upon a star,
Venus, Crawford, or Lamarr,
With sock in hand I had to mend,
I wished like hell this war would end.

There was a bit of poetic license used there, since Venus is a planet, and Crawford and Lamarr were two movie stars of that era. But it conveyed the meaning.

167

10
1945
The End of Stalag Luft 1

It was the beginning of the end. But at the time it certainly didn't feel like it. It was February and very cold. We fell out for roll call twice a day. On the coast of the Baltic it snowed often that winter, but it didn't stay on the ground very long. However, when there were snowy periods we still had to stand in formation in the snow and wait for the count to be completed. It was always accomplished by the Kommandant, his sergeant, and a number of guards.

The first Kommandant I knew walked by with his sergeant personally counting the men in each line, and this took quite a while considering how many men were in the compound. Later we got a different Kommandant who must have been at least 6-foot, 6 inches tall, and he was all legs. He strode by our formation at a terrific speed and accomplished the count in a remarkable time. We called him "Sea Biscuit" after the well known race horse of that era. Unfortunately as the war progressed they needed the younger men at the front, so "Sea Biscuit" was transferred to god-knows-where. Next they brought in an old Kommandant they must have dredged up from World War I. He moved very slowly and wore extremely thick "Coke bottle" eyeglasses. Not able to see very well, he stopped in front of each and every man in line and peered carefully to see that there were exactly three more men directly behind him in the formation. It seemed that each roll call took forever and we were freezing. We certainly missed "Sea Biscuit." In addition to the really old Kommandant, all of the younger guards were slowly replaced by the Volksturm. These were men too old to send to the front but still able to hold a rifle.

During the snowy periods our feet got so cold that a number of men developed frost bite. If their toes were bad enough they were allowed to stay in the barracks and were counted by a German guard that went through each barracks. I had mixed feelings - my toes weren't bad enough to warrant my staying inside,

---

from Brad Wilson's STALAG LUFT 1 P.O.W. JOURNAL

MARCH 27, 1945

FLASH! Barth, Germany: The Red Cross Parcels are in! ½ box per man! B.P. Wilson gets a cigarette parcel, but no mail! W.L. Ewert gets a food parcel and donates a pound of powdered eggs to the combine! Result - Spam and egg omelette and fried potatoes for dinner! Dee-licious! Patton dashing across Germany! It's a wonderful day here in Barth! See the morale-o-meter for results! That package label with "Lee B. Wilson" and "Redwood Valley" on it looked better than all the Red Cross parcels in existence!

APRIL 1, 1945

FLASH! More Red Cross Parcels and fourteen carloads of coal!

APRIL 4, 1945

Mess Hall in North Compound #1 burned down last night. Loss of food was not too great. Max Schmeling visited camp yesterday. Not impressed.

APRIL 13, 1945

News arrived today of President Roosevelt's death. It came amidst the news of great victories. The war must be in its final days now. It won't be long.

so I had to fall out for every roll call.

February was probably the worst month of my incarceration. There were shortages of everything. The war was going very badly for the Germans and Hitler was ordering wild commands that even his subordinates were loathe to follow through on. At one point in time, he ordered all of the POWs in Germany to be shot! According to our information (in camp at the time) we had Heinrich Himmler to thank for our lives, since he countermanded Hitler's orders. The handwriting was on the wall. The Allied victory would be complete and the Germans had enough to contend with without the murder of all the POW's on their heads. It's strange to think that I might have something to thank Heinrich Himmler for!

The Germans claimed that they did not have enough fuel to distribute any more Red Cross parcels. So February dawned bleak and grim. Our food was now just brot, cabbage, and turnips. One horse was said to have fallen on the ice and was butchered. We were given the horse meat while it lasted. The real crunch came to those smokers who were completely addicted to nicotine. One man in our room went around snatching up any cigarette butts he could find, putting the remnants of tobacco in a pipe and smoking it. I had given away all my cigarettes when they were coming in regularly, since they had little value at the time. In addition to the lack of food, we were also on tighter rations of coal for our stove. so we were both cold and hungry until the middle of March. That's when the Germans saw the end approaching very rapidly. Not only were the Allies making sweeping advances, but the Russians were approaching Berlin at great speed, endeavoring to get there before the Allies.

Quite suddenly the Germans found the fuel (or so they claimed) which they needed to bring the Red Cross packages from the coast where they had been warehoused - and over 35,000 packages were delivered all at once!

During that winter, as the Russians advanced from the east, several prison camps that were in their path had to be closed and the POWs were marched westward. Many lacked shoes and had their feet wrapped in rags. Many were sick. Most were starving, but they were moved westward. Our camp was orginally designed for 5,000 men, but by the end of the war we had over 8,000. We had men sleeping on the floors, in the halls, anyplace there was shelter. Our camp was on a peninsula jutting out into the Baltic and we were afraid the war would sweep by us and not even notice we were there.

By mid-March when the Red Cross parcels arrived mail arrived also. In those days, the Armed Forces were as much in the dark about the effects of tobacco as everyone else. So, assuming that most soldiers smoked, they had forms for the families of POWs to fill out and send in to the tobacco company of their choice together with a check to cover costs, and the tobacco companies would send six cartons of cigarettes to the soldier. My family knew I didn't smoke, but the Army said cigarettes were good for trading, etc. So, my father dutifully filled out the forms and sent me six cartons of Philip Morris. They arrived along with tons of Red Cross cigarettes for all those nicotine starved individuals and were immediately worthless for trading purposes. I remember that package and there, under my name, "L.B. Wilson." Those cigarettes were the only message I ever received from home, the only indication I had that anyone knew where I was. Even though I didn't smoke, that package of cigarettes was one of the most wonderful gifts I ever received, because it told me my family definitely knew that I was alive.

In the early days back in Compound One we had cigarette

smokers and pipe smokers in abundance in our room and, of course, the shutters on all the windows had to be shut tight until lights out at 10 p.m. So the smoke accumulated in the room until it was so thick it made a Los Angeles smog look like a clear spring day. We would play cards or chess at the table at night and often you couldn't see the face of the man across the table from you. As soon as the lights were out, you were allowed to open the shutters and drop the top window down just a few inches. The lights in the compound were on all night and as you lay there on your bunk you could see the smoke from the room pouring out in a thick stream, like the building was on fire.

As April began things started looking up. We had food and we got a personal visit from Max Schmelling, the former German world heavyweight who was defeated by Joe Louis, much to Hitler's distress. Max was on a "good will visit" and handed out 8x10 glossies of himself in his heyday. The glossies ended up, most appropriately, in the urinals. A few weeks later, Heinrich Himmler, the big man himself, visited our camp on an inspection to make sure it was in the best possible condition for the moment the Allies arrived. We saw him swishing around camp with his cape flying in the breeze behind him as he walked, the red lining flashing. He looked as tall as Sea Biscuit.

Then came the moment we had been waiting for, one that I will never forget. It was on the night of April 30th, 1945. While the war didn't officially end until May 15th that was the night it ended for us.

We had opened the shutters as usual after lights out and the light from the towers was streaming in our windows, as usual. Then, with no fanfare, the lights suddenly went out. Well, we had to see what was happening, so everybody crowded around the windows. It was a very bright moonlit night, and we could see the guards leaving the towers and walking away, each probably to his own home to see what the end of the war would bring. Somewhere in the camp somebody sang loudly and clearly, "God Bless America". This was a bit much to the cynical Kriegies, but we listened somewhat restlessly before going back to our bunks. No one risked going outside to see what was happening for fear of being shot. We just lay there in our bunks wondering now what tomorrow would bring.

They guys in my room finally dared open the door around five am. Dawn was almost breaking.

The first thing we saw when we got outside was the sight of the American flag flying over the camp. That was certainly a great sight. I have no idea where that had been stashed all these months. It was incredibly moving to look up and see it flying in the early morning breeze.

The second thing to greet our eyes – and this was nothing

---

from Brad Wilson's **STALAG LUFT 1 P.O.W. JOURNAL**

APRIL 30, 1945

FLASH! At 23:30 tonight the Germans left this camp. After turning off all the lights in the camp the guards left their towers and peace and quiet reigned after a day of explosions and trench digging. What a day!

MAY 1, 1945

Zemke in charge of camp, has contacted Russians. Colonel Spicer released!

short of a miracle – was the total absence of barbed wire. The fences were completely gone. Where had they put it? How was it disposed of? Who took it down? No one I spoke to that morning knew, and I never found out. Was it the Germans? Early rising Kriegies? No one took credit for it. But every strand of wire was gone and out of sight. We may not have been completely free at that point, but we felt free.

The first order that came down the line from the senior Commanding officer was to stay put! Arrangements would be made with the 8th Air Force to fly into the air strip at Barth and fly us all back to France. There was still a "hot" war going on south of us, especially as you neared Berlin about 100 miles to the south. In addition, the Russians were advancing and lobbing artillery fire at anything that moved. Most dangerous to us, there were countless land mines distributed around the camp to dissuade any prisoners from escaping. Despite these orders and warnings a few restless souls like Timothy Moriarty headed out.

Bud Morehead and I decided to camp out. After all those months of incarceration, what better way to sleep than out under the stars? It was the 1st of May, the weather was warm and clear, and now we could investigate what looked like a beautiful peninsula covered with pines and firs. So we packed a meal from our Red Cross parcels, took our blankets and pillows, and set out to find a place to spend the night. The nights were still a little on the cool side, so we looked around for something the Germans might have left behind. We could find no blankets, but in a nearby shed we found some strange looking tarps covered with pretty strands of material. Neither of us had ever encountered fiberglass at that time. Well, we got to know it quite well that night. After dinner, we lay down on the soft pine needles, got our blankets and pillows arranged, and covered ourselves with the blue tarps. We made it into the night, but it didn't last. About one o'clock in the morning we began to itch. It got worse. Every time we moved, a needle stuck us somewhere. Finally, before dawn we gave up, tossed the tarps aside and went back to the barracks. It took several days to get the fiberglass strands out of our blankets.

Then Bud had another idea.

At the end of the peninsula was a dairy of sorts. They had some cows in a corral, but no one seemed to be around to tend to them. So, Bud, being a farm boy from Iowa (originally), decided we should go up there, milk the cows and have some fresh milk for the first time in a year or more. Well, we went up there, looked over the place, found a bucket, and Bud and I approached a small cow that seemed a might skittish. She had no idea what our intentions were, but she didn't like them. It took us an hour to finally get her cornered where we could calm her down and Bud could try milking her. But that was the end, right there. The cow was dry. We gave up and went back to camp.

A day or so later, word came down from our C.O. that we should all start digging slit trenches alongside our barracks. The soil was sandy and light and it wouldn't be too hard, so we all took our trusty Klim cans and started using them to dig. The reason for the trenches was that the Russians were approaching and they might bombard the peninsula with artillery. We didn't consider that too likely so we were a bit lethargic in our digging. Then suddenly, less than a mile away, we heard several explosions, one right after another. Well, dirt began flying in all directions as we got those slit trenches finished. A bit later, we found out the explosions were caused by the Germans blowing up munitions at the Flak school down the road from the camp. The news came too late! The trenches were done.

The Russians arrived a few days later and were surprised to find a POW camp there. They told us if any resistance had been put up they would have leveled the whole peninsula with artillery. The Russian Colonel in charge of this advance unit didn't know what to do with us, but he didn't stay around long enough to decide. He moved his division onward to finish cleaning up German resistance in the area. A second Russian Colonel arrived and he came to the brilliant decision that we would have to be repatriated to Russia and we would be taken to Odessa on the Black Sea (a journey that would total 1,250 miles/2,007km) - by foot! We were told to pack the minimal belongings we needed, since we might have to go on long marches, and be ready to move out the next day. We were beside ourselves! The idea of this march was worse than staying a POW. The next day, things started looking up again. This second Russian Colonel had to move on with his troops before he could carry out his plan. That's when a third Russian Colonel arrived and since he had no official orders on what to do with us he decided we could stay put until he heard from Moscow. Shortly after that, a Russian Liaison Officer who knew about this prison camp arrived and started plans in motion for the 8th Air Force to fly us out.

It didn't turn out to be quite that easy. He decided we should all have passports, just to make sure no Germans would be escaping to America. This, of course, made little sense. Who carried a passport around with him during a war?

The next week everyone who could type was drafted into typing up passports for every man in camp. That was an interesting procedure. We were trying to type using a German typewriter on forms devised by the Russians. This went on for about three days and then the Russians decided, wisely, to scrap the whole exercise.

During the next two weeks we actually missed the Germans, at least in one respect. Compound Two had no indoor plumbing. The latrines were buildings about 20 feet by 40 feet built over a pit. Well, with over a thousand men using them daily, it didn't take long for those pits to fill up. While the Germans were running the camp, a truck known euphemistically as "the honey wagon" came in weekly and pumped out these pits. Now they were full and could no longer be used. Each room was given one or two small shovels and we were told to go out in the adjoining field and dig our own little holes. It could have been worse. But that's before we reckoned with the fun loving GIs who would stand out in the yard about where the fence used to be. Just watching other guys try to go wasn't enough. A few of them walked down to where the old Flak school was and found a supply of Very Pistols used to shoot off flares from aircraft or signal aircraft. The pistols were supposed to be pointed straight up, but our fun lovers shot off those rockets horizontally as close as they could get to whoever was out in the field sitting on his hole. It didn't provide for a relaxed experience!

11
1945
The Trip Home

Finally one day we were told to pack our bags and be ready to move out at 7 a.m. We didn't have to be told twice! Our duffel bags were now crammed with the "absolute necessities" we had to take home with us. I even had a German helmet in mine, plus little odds and ends of prison life that I had to take home, including an olive drab towel with my name carefully stitched on it, which had seen me through the last eight months. On the very top was my Army olive drab blanket that had kept me from freezing all winter - this would still come in handy in the very near future. Humans really are pack-rats, I thought. Here just nine months ago I was shot down with nothing but the clothes on my back, and here I am going back with a sack full of things I just have to have.

We marched in a loose formation down the country road, past the Flak school and through beautiful farming country to Barth. The narrow streets of the village were lined with Russian soldiers, young apple-cheeked kids that looked about 15 or 16 years old at the most. They were all smiling and waving at us and seemed to be saying, "We are your saviors! We delivered you from the wretched Germans!" We waved back in that wonderful feeling of camaraderie that exists among soldiers who all are fighting for the same cause.

It was a short five mile walk now that we had a goal in mind. We got to the air strip and saw B-24s circling above and landing, then taxiing along the side strip to a loading area. The pilots, fresh from the states, probably hadn't seen any missions, and were anticipating "getting a look" at Germany before heading back. We had other ideas. Those planes were loaded so fast the pilots never had time to cut their engines before they were being signaled to take off. This time, I was crammed into the bomb bay along with swarms of other POWs. The nose, the waist, the tail - anyplace there was room to stack us. We roared off the runway and started our low level flight back to - where? We had no idea where we were going. I hoped we were headed to England, but we didn't know. The flight was bumpy and we hit a few "air pockets" where I could have sworn the whole ship was going down. I said to myself, "Oh, no! Not again!" After what seemed like a very long flight we landed on an air strip in the middle of a large open plain. There were no buildings, no towns, very few trees. Only miles and miles of rolling open plain. Word got passed down through the men that we were somewhere in France. After a while a couple of miles worth of Army trucks pulled up and we all jumped on board, having no idea where we were going next, or why. There was no one there with a bull-horn to let us know what was going on.

    We traveled for several hours and finally turned down a road heavily lined with trees on one side. The trucks pulled to the side and stopped. Again, no one was telling us why we were here or where to go. We jumped out, duffel bags over our shoulders, and walked through the trees. The view opened up to - once again - miles and miles of open fields. But this time it was covered by miles and miles (and miles) of tents. Hundreds of tents. Thousands of tents. They stretched in even rows to the horizon, as far as I could see. We started wandering through them and discovered other GIs who had moved into the first tents and staked out a claim on a cot. So we hunted for a tent with a few vacancies. I finally found one, plunked down my bag on the cot, and sat down. I had no sooner done this that somebody yelled, "There's a mess hall down here!" We all jumped up and followed the crowd in a northerly direction through more miles of tents. Unfortunately,

I hadn't thought about painting a big red X on my tent. It would have been a good idea.

We finally came upon this massive circus tent that housed the mess hall. We got in line to get whatever they had and there I saw the most beautiful sight I had ever seen! WHITE bread! Snowy white! Gorgeous bread! I can no longer remember what else we had to eat that day; only that bread. But I am sure that we cleaned out the Mess Officer's food supplies, at least for that day! After that very satisfying meal it was nearly dark and we started back to our tents. I had lost all contact with anyone I knew and I didn't recognize anyone who had been in my tent with me before dinner. So I started looking. I could gauge pretty well how far I had come, but not well enough to find my tent. Especially not in the dark! I only remembered my cot was near the entrance and had my bag in the middle of it. I entered one tent after another, feeling around on each cot as I entered. All I would find was a disgruntled GI who had just fallen asleep. Finally, four or five tents later, I found one with a bag in the middle of the cot. I hoped it was mine. I lay down and went to sleep. It wasn't until the next morning when I woke up that I was able to check my duffle and verify that yes, indeed, it was mine.

At dawn there was a lot of racket as 8,000 men started toward the mess hall again! The meal from the night before seemed like a dream. Had it been real? Things were different this morning. Tables were set up out in the open and chow lines as well. We filled our plates, piling them high in real eggs. I found a seat and enjoyed every mouthful. After we ate someone directed somebody somewhere to get in line and sign their name to a roster so that the Mess Officer could verify the fact that he had served that many meals. The word was passed down and we dutifully got in line and waited to sign our names. Suddenly there was a rush toward the trees. From that point on, no one stayed in line to sign their name. Everyone headed for the trucks and boarded them quickly. They weren't going to get away without us!

We drove for another hour or more and entered the city of Lyon, rumbling down the streets slowly. French children lined the streets waving and cheering and begging for anything we had. Some of the GIs had extra cigarettes. I had given all of mine away back in camp. They tossed cigarettes out to the kids and they scrambled for them wildly. It was then I discovered that the value of cigarettes had risen once again to unbelievable heights. Some of the guys had saved the rest of their cigarettes so they could to do some trading at a later date.

After meandering through the town for some time, we arrived at the train station. Here we disembarked, found our way through the station and boarded a train that was at least pointed in a westerly direction. Again there was no one shepherding the flock - it was completely a game of follow-the-leader and we all hoped the leader knew where he was going. The coaches were old and war weary. None of the glass remained in the windows, so it was a breezy trip. We weren't packed in quite as tightly as we had been on the way east on the "Barth Express." Somewhere at the end of this long trip was home!

The train left the station about 2 o'clock in the afternoon and moved at a maddeningly slow pace. It was a pleasant, sunny day, so the breeze coming in the window felt good. We kept on a westerly course until about 7 pm. Then the train came to an abrupt halt. No city. No town. No special siding. We just stopped. Word filtered back that the trains in France didn't travel after dark for some reason tied to the war, which we thought was over. It was June, in northern France, and it was cold at night. As soon as the sun dropped out of sight, the cold set in. I didn't remember being this cold all winter in prison camp. Finally, some of the GIs pooled their wits and gathered some wood together and built a fire alongside the tracks. Further up the train other fires blossomed, and soon we had huge bonfires going from one end of the train to the other. To keep them going, the GIs found some railroad ties that weren't currently being used to support a track and donated them to the cause. We sat around those fires for most of the night. I took my old friendly olive drab blanket, draped it over my shoulders, and sat facing the fire. Soon I was baking on one side and freezing on the other. So I turned around and tried it the other way. After soaking up as much heat as I could, I wrapped the blanket tightly about me and went back in the train car to sit down and try to sleep. It only worked for a little while. Soon all of the heat was sapped out of me and I returned to the fire. That was a long night.

At dawn, there were some blasts from the train whistle and everyone got back on board. We started up again after another three hours or so; we began climbing hills and eventually rounded a curve and pulled into the small town of St. Valerie. Here we disembarked and started marching up a curved road over the hills. When we hit the summit we saw our destination. Spread out below us in a valley was another sea of tents bigger than the last one. This mobile city was temporary housing to over 50,000 repatriated GI's. This was Camp Lucky Strike.

We were finally separated into groups, officially assigned to temporary tents, and given food once again. After another night's sleep we were taken in, one at a time, to a debriefing officer and finally after waiting for more than nine months I got to tell my whole story of my last mission!! The debriefing officer was also very interested in verifying that I was who I said I was. I suspect that there could have been Germans trying to get out of Germany and to the United States one way or another. Looking back I think it was unlikely, but at the time I can understand the mindset that allowed those sorts of fears. So I gave the complete history of my experiences with the 445th Bomb Group. I still had no idea where Bud Morehead was, or Frank Smith or Jack Sherman, or anyone else I had known in camp. We had all been separated in the madness. They were out there somewhere in the midst of 50,000 other GIs.

The next day we got in the first of many pay lines. We hadn't been paid in almost a year and we had quite a bit of back pay coming. They only paid us about a month's income at a time, but we had absolutely no place to spend it anyway. The whole thing could have waited until we got back to the States. But we lined up anyway, wrote down our payroll signature, and collected a wad of cash. Well, it felt good anyway to have that money in my pocket anyway. It made me feel... more normal.

The nights I spent in those temporary quarters were, at best, miserable! We were sleeping in canvas tents in mummy bags. I hadn't had the horrible mummy-bag experience since that first night in Ireland some time ago. That was bad enough, but the wind at night blew in our tent and sucked all the warmth out of our bodies, and it was as cold or colder as the night alongside the train tracks. Finally one genius decided that slowing down the breeze under the cot would help to keep that from happening, He got a daily newspaper, on sale in the camp, and hung newspaper down all around the sides of the cot to keep the breeze out and weighted the newspaper down on top with the sleeping bag. It helped, but not a whole lot.

Eventually we were moved out to our "permanent" residence in another part of the sea of tents about a mile away, which was hardly any different from the "temporary" ones. Here, however, I studied the landscape carefully and identified the location of my tent. I didn't want to lose it again.

We stayed in our new residence for a full month before we shipped out for home. Most of my month in France was spent wandering all over the Camp Lucky Strike looking for familiar faces. This tent city wasn't built on flat land, but on gentle rolling hills. Every now and then Iu would come across a big Red Cross tent where they were serving special beverages, like milk shakes or fruit juice, or something else that the mess hall didn't serve. They also had chairs and books and magazines to read. One day I ran across a line that stretched over the next couple of hills and I asked what the attraction was. Well, that day it was chocolate shakes and they were serving them as fast as possible, but the line had backed up over two hills. I joined the line and soon had about a hundred more guys behind me. While we were moving along ever so slowly, Jack Stidham, my old radio man from Don's crew came running up to me, grabbed me in a bear hug and almost smothered me. He hadn't known that I survived my plane crash and was overwhelmed to see me alive and apparently well. We talked about our crashes and I told him Frank Smith had been in camp with me and was somewhere in this throng. He said he would try to find him and went off in the general direction that I indicated was the most likely place to find him. I waited in line another hour and got up almost to the tent and they ran out of chocolate shakes.

Some of the Kriegies decided they wanted to see Paris. Well, we were told we could not leave the camp, but that didn't dissuade some that believed Paris was the city in Europe that you couldn't miss. They had no transportation and M.P.s were on the watch for any soldiers going along the roads without orders. No French hotels were allowed to accept American money, and it was just too damned cold to consider sleeping out in the country. But some of them went anyway. Later I found out that Bud was one of them, much to his dismay when he got there. They got by the road check points, but after that their luck ran out. They found no place to stay; they slept in a park and froze, and didn't even have any cigarettes to trade, which would have been better than cash. So, Bud gave up and returned within three days.

That was a long month, but it had a great prize at the end of it; a ship home! Finally, one afternoon we were told to have our things packed before we went to sleep that night, because we would be called out at 2 a.m. to be trucked down to Le Havre to embark on the *U. S. General Butner*, a troop ship that had survived the war and had just arrived from the Pacific.

At 2 am. we were awakened. We shaved and dressed and were out in formation by 2:30am. We marched to the mess hall for a very early breakfast and then picked up our duffel bags, fell back into formation, and marched to the boarding area where the trucks were to pick us up. They put us at rest, and we stood there awaiting for the trucks. A half hour passed. No trucks. By 4 a.m., still no trucks. By 4:30 all the men were spread out on the grass. It was just about dawn. As the sun rose, we warmed up a little bit, at least. This was the story of the Army, being repeated again for our benefit so that we wouldn't forget, "Hurry up and wait!" Shortly after 10 a.m. the trucks arrived, over six hours late. We boarded and the trucks rolled away. I don't remember how long that drive was, but it was long enough. We finally arrived in Le Havre at dock side, and there was the *US General Butner* waiting. At least the ship was there on time.

We didn't have to be encouraged to board hurriedly, but then we discovered that being the first to board was not necessarily the best. They boarded the GIs from the bottom of the ship up, so we found ourselves on the very bottom where we were assigned to a cot which was to be our entire home for the crossing. The cots were suspended three high, so it's a wonder there was enough air in the belly of that ship to breathe. Then we discovered another fact of life. Over 95% of the men on board were officers, and since most were 2nd lieutenants, they were all assigned to the bowels of the ship, while the much fewer 1st lieutenants and Captains were assigned to 4-man rooms on the top two decks. Bud, as it turned out, was one of them. He thought it was funny. I didn't see the humor in it.

The ship, much like our POW camp, was designed to accommodate 5,000 men. To get more soldiers home in a reasonable amount of time, they put 8,000 men on board. This meant most of the enlisted men were assigned to sleeping bags out on the open decks. It also meant that there wasn't much room for "taking a stroll" or even getting a glimpse of the ocean. I worried about possible rough seas. I needn't have. The Atlantic was as smooth as glass for all eight days of our crossing, fortunately.

Now, in order to get 8,000 men on board, we had to stay in port another 24 hours. We were all steamed up and ready to shove off. The ship was not. So we had our first sample of what to expect in the way of serving food that evening. The galley, or whatever you called it on a ship, consisted of a buffet line and a large room filled with counters at chest height where you placed your trays and ate standing up. The food was good - at least compared to what we had been eating for the past year, but we could at least sit down in POW camp.

Then we discovered something that pleased me no end. We had a brick of ice cream for dessert. But that wasn't what pleased me the most; it was the wrapper that the ice cream came in. It read "Foremost Dairies, San Francisco, California." Wow! Not only ice cream, but ice cream from home! That made me feel better about the ship. It had recently visited San Francisco to take on supplies. I was almost home!

During the ensuing eight days, there was little to do but play cards and shoot crap. Not even anything to read, if I could have found a place with enough light and room to sit down. So I spent a lot of time in my bunk or standing in line. There was a PX of sorts on one of the upper decks and if I got in the single line that formed to get in there, I could walk around the entire ship twice before arriving at the destination. Having had experience in those long lines at Camp Lucky Strike I didn't have much hope of getting to the PX and finding anything. But I got in line anyway - it was something to do. Finally arriving at the counter, I found they still had some candy bars on sale - from Britain. Well, Britain had found a way to make a product that resembled a candy bar but had no sugar. I think it was made for looking and holding, but not for eating. I bought one anyway. (I had all that money burning a hole in my pocket and nothing to buy!) I did try it. Bit into it. Then I deposited it in the nearest receptacle. Then I headed back to my bunk. I remember seeing the ocean once or twice, but only through the doorway. The deck was covered with men in sleeping bags. There was no place to even put a foot. We were told to always wear our life preservers when we went out on deck, just in case an errant u-boat came by that didn't know the war was over, or in the event a floating mine was inadvertantly discovered. These were not comforting thoughts to take back down into the hold.

On the day we were to arrive in America we were anticipating seeing the Statue of Liberty, and seeing the waving, cheering crowds greeting us from the docks; hearing the brass bands and all those sorts of things that we had seen in the movies. Our homecoming was unfortunately something very different. First of all, without telling us, the ship pulled in to Norfolk, Virginia, so never saw the Statue of Liberty. The cheering crowds must have all been up in New York. There was no one on dock side in Norfolk except a small Marine Band and a group of Red Cross Gray Ladies serving donuts and coffee (perhaps to the band members - they didn't have enough for the 8,000 men on the ship!) We had just come back from the biggest war in history. We were supposed to be "conquering heroes" returning home. And what did we get? Gray Ladies and donuts.

We were bussed and trucked to Camp Patrick Henry a few miles away, where we would be for the next two weeks while the Army sorted out its logistics on how to get us home to our various states. Camp Patrick Henry wasn't too bad. We had decent mess halls, movie theaters, a PX where we could buy things, and a telephone building. The latter housed a big room with phone booths all along the walls and a desk where operators would place your call home. It took from two to three hours for a call to go through, so I placed my call and left, returning within two hours only to wait for another two. But now I had a place to sit down and read, at least.

My call finally went through within four hours and my parents were thoroughly surprised to hear from me. We'd had absolutely no contact since the day I was shot down and they didn't even know I was back in the United States. We made immediate plans to meet in San Francisco at the old Manx Hotel on Powell Street where we had stayed so many times on our trips down to San Francisco. The date was still in question, since I had no idea when we would catch a train out of Virginia. My mother told me that my grandmother had passed away a few months after I was reported missing in action. They hadn't wanted to tell her I was missing, but the lack of mail from me made her wonder. They weren't very good at covering up how they were feeling, so she guessed the truth. She was upset that they hadn't told her. Some time later when they heard from the War Department that I was a POW they told her right away, but she thought it was a fabrication designed to make her feel better. She passed away very shortly after that. So she died believing I was dead.

Bud Morehead's family lived in Iowa, but his wife had moved to Sacramento, California, during the war, to be with her sister. So Bud made arrangements without calling her to go to Sacramento. After his luggage was properly labeled and in the hands of Army transportation he finally talked to his wife and found out she had gone back to Iowa to his folks place in anticipation of his return. His luggage went to California and he went to Iowa. We made plans to meet after we got out of the service and said goodbye at Camp Patrick Henry. My train left the beautiful Virginia countryside heading west. It wasn't exactly a wartime troop train. It consisted of sleeping coaches and dining cars from pre-war America which were old and tired. But better than anything we rode on in Europe. We had stewards who came through the coaches and made up the beds every morning and put new fresh white sheets on every night. That was very nice, since we were traveling behind an old coal burning steam engine that belched out tons of smoke laced with pellets of soot. The soot filtered through the cracks and crevices and those beautiful white sheets were completely streaked with gray by morning. Meanwhile, the soot was also collecting on our clothes and in our hair and we could do nothing about that.

It was an interesting trip across country. There was no observation car, but someone had placed a couple of folding chairs in the vestibule at the end of the last car and I could go out there and sit on one of those chairs and watch the scenery falling behind me as the wheels "clickety clacked" west. The train just wasn't going fast enough. I thought of our swift trip east from Lincoln,

Nebraska, to Grenier Field, New Hampshire, and the flight overseas. It was pretty great sitting in the nose of our shiny new B-24 and flying over all that beautiful country. The only problem was we were heading the wrong way. Now that we were going home the Army was in no great hurry to get us there, so we went by train.

  I'll always remember Ogden, Utah, with great affection. That's where we dumped the coal burner and were hitched up to a diesel. No more soot! Of course that did nothing for our personal cleanliness, but at least we didn't get any dirtier. At some point I called home again and gave my parents the exact date I would reach San Francisco, so I anticipated they would be there when I arrived. At noon on the day before I got to San Francisco we stopped on top of the Sierra Nevada Mountains at the little town of Portola. They served us lunch there. I remember that well, because it was the last meal I had for the next 24 hours. The train pulled in to Camp Beale near Sacramento about 9:30 that evening. Here we were given a choice. Those of us going to San Francisco could either eat at the mess hall or take a shower. There wasn't time to do both as we had to catch a Greyhound. Frank Smith was with me. He was on his way to Oakland, but he would be on the same bus with me. We both opted to take a shower. Our hair was so thick with soot that we couldn't get a comb through it.

  We showered and shaved and put on clean clothes and headed for the bus station. Here Frank found a vending machine with some really old sandwiches in it. We tried them anyway. The bus was very slow, made many stops, and I didn't get into San Francisco until about 7 am. There was no sleep for either of us that night. I grabbed my luggage and headed for the Manx Hotel where I found a reservation had been made for me. I went up to the room, flopped on the bed and was asleep in minutes. The next thing I knew, I awoke as I heard the sound of keys in the lock and the door opening. Someone was entering the room. I propped myself up on one elbow and opened one eye. My mother and father walked into the room, laughing, smiling and crying at the sight of me. I simply said "Hi!" and collapsed back down onto the bed. My mother said, "Well, I expected a better reunion than this!"

My father was so happy to see me he just didn't know what to do. So he took me down to Samuel's, a leading San Francisco jeweler, and bought me a beautiful amethyst ring (my birthstone).

We drove home from San Francisco and my mother insisted I get out at the mail box on the county road and wait to see if Snuffy, my dog, would recognize me. Well, hadn't stood there more than thirty seconds when he came running out and leapt at me from eight feet away. He danced in circles around me and jumped all over me. I was certainly awake now!

And with that it was all over. The whole war was like a movie, playing in my mind; almost as if it had happened to someone else. I was right back where it all began. I had no idea whether or not I would have to serve in the Pacific, since the war with Japan was still going on there. I was home on a sixty day leave before I had to report to Santa Monica, which at the time was a beautiful seaside community adjacent to Los Angeles (not so beautiful anymore!) My family gathered together that first night to hear everything I had to tell them and at first it was hard to talk about our last mission and the disappearance of Teddy and the three gunners. I realized that I had never talked about that to anyone except the debriefing officer in France. Now that I finally had an audience, I got all choked up about the experience.

The Army had given all of the returning POWs hundreds of red points and blue points (needed to buy food which was still being rationed.) So my mother could for the first time in several years grocery shop to her heart's content and get everything she possibly needed. I don't believe she ever got to use all those points, because a few weeks later rationing suddenly ended. But we had a great 60 days, with the entire family getting together frequently. In

I can still remember - vividly - the day in August, still on leave, when my mother was sorting through a pile of clothes fresh from the laundry. I saw a military shirt, pulled it out and decided to iron it myself. I was in the midst of ironing that shirt when a news bulletin broke through the music on the radio. The United States had just dropped an "Atom Bomb" on Hiroshima and the war had taken a giant step to completion. Shortly thereafter, another bomb was dropped on Nagasaki and within days Japan had agreed to unconditional surrender. Now it really was all over. It was hard to believe.

With the war finally finished, why was I supposed to report to Santa Monica? Well, the Army had its inscrutable plans. When my leave was over I took the train down the Pacific coast to Los Angeles and then a bus to Santa Monica. We reported to the "Del Mar Club," a resort that was the center of our next "Sixty-day rehabilitation." We were housed in several hotels along the beach. I was in the "Shangri La," about three blocks from the Del Mar. The Officers' Mess was the plush dining room of the Del Mar, and we swam and surfed daily at the beach there. Frank Smith was there with his wife. All married officers had their wives or families with them. It was a very pleasant sixty-day rehab program.

Our pay checks still hadn't caught up with us. Now every time the local finance office received updated pay records we had another pay day. Often this would happen a couple of times a week! I sent most of mine to my bank in Ukiah, but I felt naked if I didn't have at least $200 in my wallet at all times - and in those days $200 was at least a month's pay! We felt rich!

During this time I don't remember considering the future

much. We were just enjoying each day. After several years of living day-to-day, never knowing what the future would bring, it was a frame of mind that would be hard to shake. After sixty days in this paradise we were given orders to report to (of all places) Santa Ana Army Air Base. That's where it all started. Here we went through a host of lectures and meetings to inform us of our upcoming choices. We were in the Army until the Army decided it was time to release us. Now, apparently, it was time. But they were loathe to let us go. So they gave us all kinds of options, if we stayed in. We could be transferred from the Army of the United States, a wartime organization, to the United States Army, the regular standing Army of the country. This offered us all kinds of perks, but evidently wasn't enough to draw many men to sign up for another three years or longer. The second choice was to remain in the Army Reserve, just in case we were ever needed at some future time. This offered us training opportunities, and reservists pay. The very last choice was complete and total separation.

I chose the Army Reserve. And this choice didn't make any difference in the ensuing years. It seems as though more men chose the Reserves than they had need for. So I were never called up for active training. The country was slowly sliding back into a peacetime mode where the need for a large standing Army, or even reservists, was not recognized. After two or three weeks of filling out endless forms and getting several complete physicals to make sure I was fit to turn loose, I got my separation papers and headed back on a train actually going north from Los Angeles. How refreshing.

I arrived in San Francisco to find there was a Greyhound Bus strike going on. I was supposed to pick up the train for Ukiah in San Rafael across the Golden Gate Bridge from San Francisco and now there was no bus running to take me there. After several conversations with the Army office in San Francisco, I managed to once again get on board an Army truck heading for Hamilton Air Force Base, on the outskirts of San Rafael. I was told that once there I could get their transportation office to furnish me a ride to the train station.

I had to be at the train station by a certain time, but the Army, being what it is, doesn't go by any other departure times but its own. I talked to the transportation office at great length and they promised me a ride to the train station, but I must just be patient. Well, about an hour later, they told me I should get on a truck with a bunch of other officers that were also leaving about the same time. I was the last one on the truck - me and my baggage. Then, as the truck rolled away, I found we were all heading for the airstrip where these men were boarding a plane bound for China. Of course, we went to the air strip first, and I had to disembark in order to let all the other men and their baggage off the truck. This left me standing on the runway like a guy who was waiting for the next plane to Peking! I was urged to board the plane quickly several times and had to convince them I wasn't going. After everyone who was China bound boarded the plane I buttonholed the driver and reminded him he also had a passenger for San Rafael. He reluctantly agreed and we finally went to the train station where, fortunately, my train was still waiting.

When I got home this time, I felt relieved and let down at the same time. For the last three years, I had a pretty good idea what was coming next. Now I had to plan my own future.

12
1997
An Anniversary

On July 9th and 10th, 1997, my wife Joy and I were in San Francisco celebrating our 49th anniversary. Imagine, forty-nine years! On the 9th my friend Bill Kenworthy, who used to work on the *Ukiah Daily Journal* with me, came up to San Francisco and stayed at the same motel with us. We went to dinner together and then went to a movie. The movie theatre was an old one on North Point and it closed permanently right after that run. (When Bill was visiting us in Pollock Pines we went to a restaurant called "Weird Harold's" for dinner. Shortly after that, "Weird Harold's" closed permanently, too. Bill wrote me and said, "We've got to be careful which places we go!")

The next morning we had breakfast together and toured the Ghirardelli Square area (we'd done Pier 39 the day before), and then he left for home. We spent the rest of the day and evening there and left for home the next morning after driving over Nob Hill and admiring the old apartment house where I lived over 70 years ago. It has held up very well. Don't know about the interior, though. When we lived there, every time a tenant moved out they had the apartment re-painted until the coats of paint built up about an inch thick! By now, the layers of paint might have filled up the entire apartment!

In January, 1946, I started college at Santa Rosa JC. I wasn't about to get stuck back home again. LB was all for it, but Noan, of course, was upset to have me gone again so soon. When I came home two years later and announced that I was getting married, that was fine with LB, but Noan had to query me about every aspect to make sure this girl was qualified for her son. Of course, I brought my wife-to-be up to see them several times over the school year to get them used to the idea of seeing her around. Bebe Snow fell in love with her and told me not to let her get away.

When we got married LB had his favorite carpenter build a little three room bungalow adjoining the vineyard on his property. (Probably with Noan egging him on.) This was ours to use whenever we were in Redwood Valley and could be sort of a "home base" for us while we were still in college.

LB smoked, which didn't enhance his longevity. He also had a few drinks each day. Neither one of these things helped his longevity. But, he looked so very good that it was deceiving.

After I went to work at NASA's Ames Research Center in 1958 he went to the hospital a few times and ended up being diagnosed with incurable cancer. He lived long enough to meet his three grandchildren; Perry, Brook and Crystal, but died in 1963, at the age of 73.

My mother, Noan, barely outlived him, and passed in 1965. My family, which had seemed so big when I was a child, was reduced to just myself and my cousin Virginia. So I started my own. And now I have my wonderful wife, my three great kids, and three beautiful grandchildren.

Editor's Postscript

Here my father's written story ends. He intended to write more, but he always thought the later years would be less interesting to whomever was "forced to read" his story. At Santa Rosa Junior College he met my mother, Joy Carolyn Frerichs, and they married in 1948. He attended Stanford University for a brief time and then moved back to Ukiah to help care for his parents. They built a house (doing all of the work themselves) and he paid the bills working in a camera shop and as an advertising salesman for the Ukiah Daily Journal.

In the late 1950s he got a civil service job working for the U.S. Army and then NASA at the Ames Research Center in Mountain View, California. I was born and shortly thereafter my brother Brook and sister Crystal.

Brad retired in 1981 and he and my mother did a lot of traveling. He wrote a number of detailed travel diaries – sailing through the Panama Canal, visiting Australia, New Zealand, and every island in the Caribbean. They drove across the North American continent more than once, taking a long trip through Canada. He didn't bother to chronicle the dozens of cruises or trips to Hawaii to visit his only living relative other than his wife and children - cousin Virginia Huber, who died in 2000.

He now has four grandchildren; Crystal's daughters Jessica and Megan, my daughter Alexandria, and Brook's son Tyler Bradford Wilson, who Brad didn't get a chance to meet - but if he had he would have thought his namesake grandson was a pistol!

AFTERWORD

On December 3, 2007, my father left a note on the refrigerator for my mother, who was still asleep; "Lots of things to do today, be back late." He drove into town to get an oil change, see the doctor, and do some grocery shopping. Around 2:00pm he was hit by a van while crossing the street (in a crosswalk). I was at work when I received a call from the hospital and hurried to the Emergency Room. He passed at about 4:00pm.

I personally found it stunning that - after living through being shot down, parachuting through enemy fire, and enduring prison camp - he was killed walking through town while on a day of errands.

Just the day before my wife, daughter and I had taken him with us to a Christmas Tree Farm and he had climbed the hill to pick out the very best tree. We went to lunch together and he passed on pizza because he was trying to eat only healthy foods.

My family gathered at the hospital that night. Eventually, once arrangements were made, we left and took my mother home. I put away the groceries my father had purchased on his last day. My mother finally fell asleep, no doubt still in shock. I stayed with her, trying to sleep on the spare bed in my father's office. Sleep proved impossible, so I turned on his computer in order to compose an e-mail reporting his death which I would send out to friends and family members the next day. Opening his Documents folder I found, right at the top, a folder called "Notes to Perry." It might have been something old, a note he had sent me long ago and never deleted. But at that moment I needed for him to speak to me, and here was a personal note written directly to me.

AFTERWORD

So I opened it. There were some Living Trust files, bank information files, and one called "Perry - Read This.doc."

It read:

Dear Perry,

    Since I won't be around to guide you, this is a "what to do Letter" to lead you through the confusion of tying up loose ends of a lifetime.

    Looking back, (I'm about to reminisce - again), over the last 80 some years (at this point in time), I've had a very pleasant life. Nothing earth-shaking, but pleasant. I had a sort of "fantasy" existence during my early years in Almaden, a really exciting place to live from the age of five to thirteen, then a great country life during my high school years in Redwood Valley. There were no drugs in those days and life was good.

    World War II came along at just the right time (if it had to come at all) - I hadn't started a career or even college at that point. So if I ever had to go into the army it was a good time to do it. I know this may sound surprising, but the war was never really frightening. I never expected to be killed in action, but if I was, so be it. I experienced comradeship, lots of training, flying in all kinds of aircraft, and navigating our bomber back from a mission where we lost two engines and had to drop out of our group. I was delighted to guide us back to our air base after having to take several devious corridors around London, where they shot you down, allied plane or not, just because you were there, if you drifted into that no-fly-zone. Even prisoner-of-war camp, as bad as it was, was an interesting experience. We had a few scary moments, but all in all, it was sort of like Hogan's Heroes, without all the devious escape plans.

After the war, there was college, marriage, and then starting a serious-get-down-to-business life. I started working on a permanent basis on January 3, 1949. From that day on, I was never unemployed until the day I retired on December 31, 1981. So, all in all, I only worked for 32 years of my life, plus three years in the army. And as of this date, May, 2004, I have been retired for 23 years and going strong! If I keep this up much longer, I will have been retired longer than I worked!!

Now, as pleasant as this life was, that is not to say I would not do things differently if I had the chance to do it all over again. Hindsight is great – if only you had it at the beginning. I'd like to pass on to my children and grandchildren some of the wisdom that has accumulated in the deep recesses of my mind, but I seriously doubt that you would act on it. That's just not the way it is. People have to stumble through life and make their own dumb mistakes. My advice is: JUST DON'T MAKE THE SAME DUMB MISTAKES TWICE!

If there is just one thing I can pass on to you all, it is this: Your health is paramount to anything else you do in life. Eat properly, exercise daily, and, as Spock says, live long and prosper. In other words, take care.

We don't know what date we are going – but it is deeply carved in stone and there is no changing it. The only thing is, that darn day can sneak up on you suddenly and take you by surprise.

Love beyond all measure,
Pa

After the many hours it took for me to recuperate emotionally from this unexpected message I also found on his computer all of the files that comprise this book. So here I present them to let my father speak his piece and leave his story.

There have been many stories written by the veterans of World War II (a little Internet research will turn up hundreds of similar memoirs.) Yet I still think this one has its own place and message. He was the kindest and gentlest man I ever knew and a day never passes when I don't try to find a way to be a little more like him. More often than not I fail at this, but his wisdom, good humor and perseverance will influence me until my own final day, whenever that will be.

Perry Bradford Wilson
August, 2010

www.ingramcontent.com/pod-product-compliance
Lightning Source LLC
LaVergne TN
LVHW011347080426
835511LV00005B/176